Trans-Formations

From Field Boots to Sensible Heels

Erika Shepard

For more information contact:
crystalhillpubs@outlook.com

ISBN: 978-1-7350032-0-7

Published by Crystal Hill Publishing, Inc. USA

CONTENTS

CONTENTS

AUTHOR'S NOTE

A memoir relies on memory, which is often unreliable. It's always a bit out of focus, like looking through a shimmering pool of murky water to gauge the depth of the bottom.

Thus I have taken liberties; I have condensed related events to fit into a single chapter or scene; I've created dialogue from the bits and pieces I can recall to show the story as clearly as possible; I've changed the names of some individuals I encountered along the way. But as best I could, I have written the truth as I remember it.

DEDICATION

For Mom and Barb.
To Liz and Barbara and Spence.
To Olga and Mel and Redd and Beth.
And yes, you too, LaDonna.
Thank you all, each and every one.

PART ONE

Igneous

Deep within the earth lie vast chambers churning with hot molten rock called magma. Flowing in the utter darkness, the currents within carry tiny growing crystals, each taking their nourishment from the seething fluid around them. As they grow, they are swept along with other crystals in the stream, colliding with each other and the chamber walls.

On their long journey, the crystals absorb an impurity here, suffer a tiny fracture there, and in so doing each becomes unique.

Such chambers are the wombs from which mountains grow.

So it is with people. We grow from womb to life, encountering the world along the way. We each bear the scars and triumphs of our journey, and thus gain the characteristics that make each of us unique.

One

My Dog Nickie - 1953

I was five years old, and I was a boy.

They told me that because I had "boy parts." I didn't care. What I cared about was playing house in the big cardboard box Mommy brought home, and playing with my dog, Nickie. He was five years old, too.

Nickie was a German Shepherd and Collie mix with a pointy face, upright ears, and short fur. His shoulders were draped in tan and white just like a Collie. When I stood up, Nickie and I touched noses, but his was black and wet all the time and mine was dry, mostly, and turned up a little at the end. Pale-skinned and dotted with freckles, I got sunburnt sometimes, my skin turning red and hurting a lot. But worst of all, I had carrot-red hair like my Daddy had when he was little. Nobody else in my neighborhood or even in first grade had red hair.

Daddy was average size and, according to Mommy, a nice-looking man. His name was Earl, and his thick brown hair looked coppery in the sun. He worked on cars at a place he called "the shop," and when he came home he smelled like oil and grease. He always said, "Hi, Butch," when he walked in the door.

I hated that name.

Mommy's name was Margaret, and she had nice brown hair, too, only darker. When she got it curled every month, it smelled funny. Her nose was a little too big, but she was smart, and she loved me and my two younger sisters. I especially liked her eyes because they were a greenish color she said was "hazel." My eyes were that color too.

She called me Richard.

On Saturday mornings, Nickie and I always sat on the floor while we watched Howdy Doody. Afterwards, if the weather was nice, we went outside to play fetch. He would chase the ball and bring it back all slobbery and tug on old ropes or rags with me. Sometimes, though, he scared me.

When I ran he sometimes chased after me, jumping on my back and knocking me down, rubbing his front teeth on the back of my neck. I could feel the front of his fangs, but he never, ever bit me. If I cried, he stopped and licked me—my face, my ears, everywhere his long wet tongue could reach. He licked me until I laughed and laughed, trying to get him to stop. He was sorry he scared me.

I loved Nickie, even if he did scare me sometimes.

One special weekend, Daddy took me on a long trip to see his Momma and Gramps on their farm in the Ozarks. We had been there once before, but this time we took Nickie. It was going to be lots of fun, playing with him in the cornfields and the little creek down the hill from their house.

After a long drive, we finally arrived late on a cool, clear Friday night. We went straight to bed. In the morning, as I walked into the kitchen, there was a serious discussion going on among the adults gathered around the breakfast table. They stopped talking as soon as I sat down.

Daddy didn't look right, so I asked, "What's wrong, Daddy?"

"One of our farm geese was killed last night, Butch. We think Nickie did it."

"Oh."

I didn't know what else to say. I was sorry it happened and sad that we would probably have to go home.

While I ate my cornflakes, Daddy slipped away with Gramps and went to the barn. For some reason Daddy didn't want me play outside that morning, so I stayed inside and read my book. It was about Dick and Jane.

It was really boring.

It was at lunch that, after I finished my peanut butter and jelly sandwich, Daddy turned to me and said in a rough voice, "Get in the bedroom and shut the door."

Wide-eyed, I scurried to the bedroom, sitting on the bed next to the window. What did I do? Why is Daddy mad at me, I wondered? A few minutes later a rumbling noise rose up from the old rusty farm tractor I had seen in the barn.

Peering out through the dirty, torn screen on the window, I watched as my Daddy got on the tractor with Gramps. Both of them carried big guns. The tractor pulled a flat cart behind it. Nickie and one of their dogs were on the cart trying to balance, leashes around their necks tied to the rails.

The tractor turned out of the yard, chugging down the sloping road next to the cornfield toward the creek about a half mile away. I strained at the window, trying to see what they were doing, but it was too far.

5

Why couldn't I go to the creek, too? Did I do something wrong? Why did they take the dogs?

It seemed like forever when, suddenly, two loud blasts boomed from down by the creek.

No! It can't be! I thought, terrified. Maybe they just went hunting or something! Maybe the dogs scared up an animal and they shot at it!

I stared out the window for like a million years. Finally, the tractor reappeared, grinding back up the slope toward the house. Nickie and the other dog were lying on the cart behind the tractor. They were all bloody. They were dead. Daddy had killed Nickie. He had shot him with a gun.

"Why?" I bawled when he walked through the door. "Why?"

Daddy looked at me, his face hard. "Can't have a bird killer around. And quit crying like a little girl, dammit!"

But I couldn't stop crying. On Sunday, we went home

Two

The Studebaker - 1955

I stepped off the school bus into the sticky Kansas heat in front of my house. Immediately I could hear that Mommy and Daddy were arguing inside. Not again, I thought.

Clutched in my sweaty hand was a picture I had drawn in my class for Mommy. It had a bright yellow sun, a blue streak for the sky, and a white puffy cloud drifting over our house. A small face looked out the window. It was not a happy face.

The hot, white sidewalk led to a steep stairway in front of our house. At the bottom I paused, then took a deep breath and trudged up the steps. Reaching the wooden screen door, I tried to slip inside. Immediately my father's voice bellowed at me, hitting me like heat from Mommy's oven.

"Go to your room, dammit!" He stood next to the kitchen counter in his greasy work clothes, his face ruddy with anger. Mommy sat at the kitchen table, eyes red from crying.

I hurried around the corner to the bedroom where my younger sister Brenda perched on the edge of her bed, eyes wide. She was three, with brown hair like Mommy. My youngest sister, Barbara, one-and-a-half years old, sat in her crib in the corner, quiet but wide awake. She had red hair like me.

I jumped onto my bed on the other side of the room, cramming myself into the corner. When Daddy pounded on the counter with his fist I could feel it in the wall.

What is it this time?

Oh.

Daddy has bought a used car—a Studebaker—without asking Mommy, and she doesn't like it. Mommy says Daddy doesn't make a lot of money.

"It's a damn good car! It just needs a little fixing," Daddy growled.

"I don't care how good you think it is," Mommy fired back. "We can't afford it!"

It always felt like something bad was going to happen at our house. We didn't know what, but we knew it would hurt, one way or another.

Arguments were part of it. They started on one thing, but soon Daddy would yell about everything: Mommy's housekeeping, her cooking, whatever. It didn't matter. Inevitably he'd get around to us—"her" kids.

"Those stinkin' brats of yours, they're stupid little shits and don't know enough to clean up after themselves. And that boy: he's a sissy, dammit! Do you hear me? He needs a good whippin' to make a man of him!"

"They're just fine, including Richard, no thanks to you!"

I didn't understand why Daddy didn't like me playing house or drawing pictures and stuff. He said he wanted me to be a Real Man. I didn't know what that was, but I knew I wasn't doing it right.

I played catch and other things like that when I had to, but I really wanted to play with my sisters or the neighbor girls. Better yet, I liked to build houses out of big cardboard boxes and play in them, arranging the rooms and windows. I collected pieces of wood or buckets to make pretend furniture. Then I drew pictures on the inside walls of the box with my crayons, pictures of flowers and sunny landscapes, the sky a blue streak across the top just like the picture I had brought home for Mommy.

Daddy yelled louder now. "What's this crap I hear about him playing house like some damn interior decorator? What the hell will the neighbors think? He's a sissy, woman! Dammit, can't you do your fuckin' job?"

His words shook the walls, spewing out the open windows into the world for all to hear. It scared me. Would Daddy hit Mommy? Would he come in here and hit me? But Mommy kept fighting back. Oh Mommy, be careful!

Suddenly there was silence—then, clear and loud, we heard Daddy thunder: "I've had it, bitch! I'm outta here!" With that, he stomped out the front door, slamming it behind him.

In the awful quiet that followed, Mommy sobbed.

I did not understand. What had just happened? Is Daddy coming back? Where is he going?

Doesn't Daddy love us anymore?

As tears streamed down my face, I looked over at Brenda. Her cheeks were wet with tears, too, as she stared at me.

At that moment it hit me. This horror, all of it, was my fault.

The yelling, the crying, Daddy leaving, was all my fault—because I was a sissy.

TRANS-FORMATIONS

Three

The Railroad Tracks - 1956

D addy never came back, so our lives changed.

We moved to Kansas City, Missouri. Mommy found work with the federal government as a secretary, but her salary was not enough to take care of us. So her father, the one we called Grampa, bought an old two-bedroom house in a working-class part of town and a cheap car for us. Even though he bought these things, I didn't like him.

Grampa was a high school mathematics teacher. He had been teaching the same classes for more than thirty years. Tall and gaunt, he had deep lines on either side of his large, hooked nose. He looked almost like a stick figure, I thought, the kind I drew with crayons when I was little. He always wore old clothes when he came to check on us, threadbare and stained, just hanging off him. He smelled sour all the time and never smiled.

Our Gramma, who was paralyzed by a stroke, was nice, but she had died a few months earlier. I thought it made Grampa sad, but I couldn't tell. He never said anything about it.

Grampa didn't throw anything away because he lived through the Depression, Mommy said. He saved bent nails in jars and pieces of wire and string wrapped around sticks that he kept in his dark, musty basement. She said he was not poor, but that he sent lots of his money to a club called the John Birch Society. His house had piles of their special newspaper. I tried to read it once, but he took it away when I asked a question about some man named McCarthy who was looking for Commies.

It was a stupid newspaper anyway. There weren't any comics.

Even though he didn't live with us, I think Grampa believed that because he owned the house we lived in and the car we used, he owned us, too. He told us what to do, and I sometimes heard Mommy and him arguing.

Since we moved, Grampa insisted I take the streetcar to a school near his house instead of the one in our neighborhood. He told me I had to be "the man of the house now," and needed to learn responsibility. I just thought it was neat that I got to ride the streetcar to school all by myself. Brenda and Barbara didn't go to school yet, so they had to stay all day at the babysitter's house across the street while Mom was at work.

But today was Saturday, and I wanted to go outside.

"Mom, can I go down to the railroad tracks?"

"Yes, but be home for supper. That's in about two hours, okay?"

I dashed outside, letting the wooden screen door slam behind me. I ran up our short gravel driveway and down the lumpy asphalt street toward the railroad tracks about a quarter mile away. Sweat trickled down my back under my tee shirt as I jumped over dusty potholes and cracks in the hot black surface. I loved being away from our little house. Outside, I was free. I could breathe.

The rail line was on a raised embankment. It was where I caught the streetcar to go to school, so I knew it well. Climbing the well-worn path along the slope to the top, I looked around.

To the left, the hot iron rails dwindled to a shimmering point in the distance. To the right, they bent around a curve about a half-mile away. It was there, just the week before, that I'd found some interesting rocks between the railroad ties. Some sparkled, some were different colors. I wanted to find more.

I turned left. Walking slowly, head bent, I stepped from rail tie to rail tie, scanning the gravel between them from side to side. The summer heat reflected off the rocks, making me squint in the brightness. The oily smell of warm creosote filled the air, along with the faint calls of birds and the clickity-clickity sound of grass-hoppers as they jumped from one patch of tall yellow grass to an-other.

Most of the rocks between the ties were a light gray color, lo-cal rocks that were found nearly everywhere in town. Sometimes, though, a bright glint caught my eye, and I eagerly stopped to pick up the shiny object. Usually it was a disappointment: a single tiny crystal face with no particular shape, or a bottle cap half buried in the gravel. But after about twenty minutes, a different kind of reflection caught my eye.

Nestled in the gray gravel was a rock I had never seen before. It was shaped like the sugar cookies Mom sometimes made for us. It was covered with tiny flat silvery crystals. It glowed with a sheen like satin in the sun. I picked it up and nestled it in the palm of my hand. It felt warm there, almost alive.

Where did it come from, I wondered? What kind of rock is it?

I dropped to my knees, searching for more like it, digging through the loose gravel with my hands. In the next hour I found two gray rocks with nice little crystals. Once, the streetcar rumbled by; I waved to the driver and he rang the bell for me. Finally, the sun moved west, so I turned toward home, anxious to show my Mom the wonderful thing I had found.

"Mom," I yelled as I banged through the front door, "I found a cool rock!" Proudly I showed her my new acquisitions, babbling about my discovery.

"That's nice, Richard," she said, examining my finds with a smile. "But supper's ready now, so go wash your hands."

"Okay," I said. But before washing my hands I held the stone in my hand for a moment. It was still warm. Reluctantly, I wrapped the rocks in toilet paper and put them in the special shoebox I kept under my bed.

The following Tuesday Mom gave me a surprise: my very own paperback copy of *The Golden Book of Rocks and Minerals*.

"Wow, Mom, thanks!" I ran to my room and pulled the shoe box from under the bed, quickly flicking through the pages, thinking—it's gotta be here somewhere!

Four

The First Time - 1956

The bright summer sun and blue skies of July had passed, replaced by the sullen gray drizzle of October. Now in third grade, I still commuted to school by streetcar each day.

I didn't mind. Some afternoons when the weather was nice I walked the 17 blocks from school to home along the tracks, looking for more rocks and saving the ten-cent fare in the process.

It was Saturday, and as was often the case when the weather was bad, I spent the day across the street playing at Karen's house. She was the only kid my age who lived nearby. She was plump with wavy brown hair cut short, deep brown eyes, and a pleasant way about her. She was one of those smart girls you knew would someday wear glasses and run an office or be a nurse.

Her parents were nice too. Her dad would kindly fix my bike when I brought it to him, even if it wasn't really broken, and her mom made cookies for us on rainy days, usually chocolate chip. We sat at the kitchen table with a glass of milk to eat them.

On this day, we played Monopoly and Sorry all morning as we lay on her living room floor, but the games had gotten old and boring. Barely able to suppress our giggling, we tried calling a

15

drug store on the phone, asking, "Do you have Prince Albert in a can?"

The druggist who answered just laughed and said, "Yes!"

Apparently, he had heard that one before.

As we tried to decide what to do next, Karen suddenly lit up. "Hey, let's play dress-up!" she exclaimed. "We've got a box of clothes in the basement that's going to be donated this week."

Not quite sure what she had in mind, I followed her down the stairs leading to the basement. It was a dim space, with just a couple of yellowish light bulbs hanging from the ceiling. It smelled of dust and laundry detergent.

"The box of clothes is over by the washer. You get it and I'll get my dishes out of my toy chest!"

Dutifully, I dragged the box over to where Karen crouched down on an old carpet spread on the concrete floor, digging through a pink plastic toy chest, pulling out plastic cups and saucers.

"We can pretend like we just met and are having tea," she said. "We'll both be women!" With that, she stood up and began rummaging through the clothes box.

"Here it is!"

She straightened up, holding in her hands a wrinkled cotton dress in a style that reminded me of one my Mom wore. A deep royal blue with white buttons down the front and short sleeves, it came with a matching cloth belt.

"It's a shirtdress," she explained. "Here, take off your t-shirt and roll up your jeans. You put it on over your head."

"Uhh, okay."

Halfheartedly, I slipped off my t-shirt and rolled up the legs of my jeans, as instructed. As I pulled the dress over my shoulders, Karen stepped up and adjusted it, helping me with the buttons. She then turned to the box, looking for something for herself.

She found a beige twill skirt and dark blue sweater. She put them on, then sat arranging the cups and saucers on the carpet. "Let's pretend we're grown-up women and that we're having tea," she said, smiling. "You can tell me all about yourself, and I'll do the same."

I sat down on the carpet, cross-legged, knees poking out from under the dress.

"No," she said, "you've got it wrong. Sit like this."

She adjusted both her legs to one side, then arranged her skirt over them, spreading it as much as possible. It felt awkward, but I did as she showed me.

She settled into position, then extended her hand toward me. "Hello, my name is Karen. What's yours?"

I hesitated for a moment, then picked the first name that occurred to me. "My name is Patricia," I replied. There was a cute girl in my class at school by that name.

"Pleased to meet you," she said. "Would you like some tea?"

"Uh, yeah. I mean, yes, thank you." I realized my heart was pounding. Why? I asked myself.

But I knew why. I very well knew why.

Karen went through the motions of pouring tea for each of us, then asked me, "Sugar or milk, Patricia?"

"Just sugar, please."

Karen stirred in an imaginary spoonful of sugar, then handed me the cup and saucer. "Well, I'll tell you about myself first, then it will be your turn."

Karen began, weaving a story of her imaginary husband and their perfect lives. He, like her father, was an engineer. They met at college, she said, and now lived in a beautiful three-bedroom house in a lovely neighborhood with trees and parks. She wove a fairy tale story of a balanced, happy household with two parents who loved their child, parents who hoped to someday add a little brother to the family.

It was a foreign land to me, lovely and unreal.

"Now it's your turn, Patricia. Tell me about yourself," she said, sitting back.

I took a deep breath, and jumped over the cliff.

"Well, I am twenty-seven years old too. I've got pretty blonde hair and I don't have any kids 'cause my husband died in a terrible accident. I work in a jewelry store, but I'm the manager 'cause I know a lot about rocks and minerals."

"No you're not! Girls can't be managers!"

"Yes I can," I replied, indignant, "because I am one and it's my story."

"Oh, all right," she grumbled, frowning.

I started again, and in a lightning flash the realization struck me—it was so simple, so easy. I could paint my life with words. I could be anyone I wanted.

And I wanted to be a girl.

Time slowed as my surroundings suddenly came into focus, a sudden clarity in the dimness of the dark basement. I sensed a faintly sweet scent rising from the dress. I could hear the light rain outside, pattering against the dirty window over the wash-er. Beneath my bare legs, the rug under the spread-out dress felt rough and scratchy, but the fabric of the dress was soft and cool. My legs ached from their unusual position.

I rushed on, driven, leaping from my heart into this new and exciting world.

"Last year my store did well and the company gave me this necklace as a reward. Isn't it pretty?"

I pretended to show Karen the pearl necklace. She leaned forward and looked. "That's just lovely, dear. How nice of them!"

For eons it seemed, we spoke of home décor and babies, diamonds and curtains and pictures on the wall. In that imaginary time, that dark sweet basement glowed with wondrous images drawn with bright color and clear light, with pure love and warm contentment. We, both of us, wove our lives from the hopes inside us, wove them from hopes and dreams that we thought would be ours, even then. Mine, so very unexpected, welled up of its own accord from a place I hadn't known existed. I wanted, with every bone, every fiber, every thought—to be a girl.

We slowed toward the end of the afternoon, each embracing the moment in our own private ways.

This is wonderful, I thought, and for a long, delicious moment, my head tilted back, my eyes closed, I immersed myself in the absolute joy of it. Then, amidst the silkiness of the dress, amidst the sweet fragrances of perfume and laundry soap, there arose a dangerous, utterly forbidden thought—I AM a girl.

In a lightning moment, stabbing me like a dagger to the throat, came also this; Daddy was right about me.

The next weekend it rained, and again Karen and I played at her house. After an hour or so of board games, I quietly asked her, "Do you still have the clothes in the basement?"

"No," she replied. "We took them to Goodwill on Monday."

Devastated, I tried not to show it. All week I had been re-living our afternoon in my mind, hoping the clothes would still be there one more time. We continued our board game, but I couldn't concentrate.

I pondered how an old dress from a cardboard box in a musty basement had opened the door to feelings I didn't understand, feelings that made me want to cry and laugh in the same moment. For a short time, I had felt alive, free.

I sat staring down at the Monopoly board, while a single word whirled in my mind, screaming round and round, growing louder and louder.

Sissy. Sissy. Sissy.

Five

Captain Mom - 1957

September, and the air was crisp with the smells of fall. Maple leaves in their millions were giving up their summer colors, their deep velvety greens fading to reveal brilliant shades of red and orange, while elms turned to a soft, buttery yellow, all falling to the ground in a multi-colored flurry with the slightest breeze. It was the time when, in the early mornings, frost glistened on the grass in the slanted pale light of the rising sun. The earth was preparing for winter.

I sat on the floor of the living room, rummaging through the bottom drawer of the tall antique secretary that had been in our house since I could remember. It held the papers and records of the family and a few keepsakes. There was a sepia photograph of Grampa, stern and upright, standing next to Gramma before she had the stroke. There was one of Mom when she was a little girl. She was cute in a tomboy kind of way, her dark brown hair cut in a page boy, setting off the lacy white dress she wore for the occasion. She looked just like Brenda. There was a picture of Dad too, in an Army uniform. It showed no rank, carried no medals. I didn't ask about him, although I looked at it for a long time. Vaguely, I wondered why I felt nothing.

Then something else caught my eye.

"Hey Mom, what's this?"

"It's my pilot's logbook, honey," she replied from the kitchen.

"Really? You flew airplanes?"

"I didn't just fly, honey, I taught people to fly. That was before you were even born."

Carefully, I opened the thin, dark green book to peer at the tiny writing inside.

"What does this mean?" I asked.

Mom pulled out a kitchen chair and carried it over to sit next to me. Her hair fell to one side of her face, brushing my neck as she leaned close to look over my shoulder. She smelled faintly of perfume, overlain by the warm fragrance of mashed potatoes and gravy. Mom-smells.

"Well, this column is where you write in the date of your flight. The next ones are for the type of airplane and its registration number. Then it shows where we took off and landed, and any comments about what we did along the way. The last columns are used to count the number of hours of flight time and how many landings we made."

"You were teaching people all the time?"

"Not always, honey. Sometimes it was just me practicing. It's one of those things you have to keep practicing to stay safe. But most of the time, I taught people to fly, and many of them, young men mostly, went on to fly in the military."

"Wow!" My mom was the coolest mom ever, and I hadn't even known it!

"Could you take us up in an airplane?"

"No dear, I haven't flown in a long time," she said as she straightened up. "But you know, I've been thinking about joining the Civil Air Patrol so I can fly again. They have airplanes. If I join, would you like to come to a meeting?"

"Cool!"

A few weeks later Mom went to her first meeting. She came home that evening happy and excited, telling us she was going to join the local "squadron." She said she would go to meetings one night a month.

As time went on, she got more involved and was awarded the rank of Captain. She had a uniform and everything! We were almost as excited as she was about this new adventure.

It was good to see her happy.

True to her word, she got permission to bring me along to some of her meetings at the airfield. While she attended, I played in an old airplane hulk parked in the grass in front of the hangar. Sometimes, on rainy nights, I played inside where they had a simple flight simulator used to teach instrument flying methods. They called it a Link trainer, and they let me sit in the cockpit and pretend to fly.

Just before Christmas that year Mom arrived home after one of her meetings and called my sisters and me out to the living room. "I have a special Christmas present for all of you," she announced. "We are going on an airplane flight over the city to see Christmas lights from above!"

Our jaws hung open at the thought of such an adventure: an airplane ride just for us!

"When? What kind of airplane? When? Are you gonna fly it?" The questions came out of us in a rush.

"It's in two weeks, and I'll be co-piloting so I can get the flight hours I need. It's a big airplane with two engines, called a C-45," she grinned. "So you have to be patient for a while."

Patient? How could we possibly be patient!

Two weeks dragged on and on, but eventually the day came for our flight. In late afternoon, Mom piled us into the car and we drove to Kansas City Municipal Airport, just across the Missouri River from downtown. Pulling up next to a big hangar and shutting off the engine, she turned to us in her seat.

"Now listen. The nice man flying the plane is Captain Douglas. Be sure to say thank you. He'll tell you where to sit and show you how to work the seat belts, so pay attention. After we get into the air, we might be able to walk around inside the plane a little bit, but only if he says so. Understand?"

We nodded dutifully and piled out of the car. Mom, leading her three little chicks, guided us through the back door and into a dark, cold hangar. Although it was nearly evening outside, from inside we could see, gleaming under a spotlight outside the large, open front doors, the airplane we were going to fly over the city.

Leaning back as if ready to jump into the sky, its shining aluminum skin sported a thin red line painted along the side from nose to tail. It had two big round engines, one on each wing. The tail itself was a long horizontal piece with roundish uprights on each end emblazoned with the C.A.P. logo. The oval rear door in the side stood open, waiting for us.

A tall man in khaki pants and white shirt stepped out of a side office. Slipping on a leather jacket, he walked over to meet us.

"Hello George," my Mom said.

"Hi Margaret," he replied as they shook hands. "So this is our crew for the flight?"

Turning to us Mom said, "Yes, here they are. This is my son Richard and my daughters Brenda and Barbara. Now what do you have to say to Mr. Douglas, kids?"

"Thank you, Mr. Douglas," we replied almost in unison. He called us crew! I thought excitedly, straining to see the airplane as he spoke.

"You're welcome, kids. If you're ready, let's go over to the airplane and I'll explain some things."

We walked onto the tarmac to the side of the plane.

"Now, this plane looks similar to the one flown by Amelia Earhart, but it's made by a different company. Do you know who she was?" he asked when we stopped by the door. I nodded, knowing my sisters wouldn't know, or care.

Even so, when Mr. Douglas paused to look down at us, he realized he was wasting his breath explaining technical details. We were all goggle-eyed at the airplane, and clearly anxious to get inside.

"Okay then," he said, turning. "Ladies first!"

He mounted the short steps extending out of the plane and turned, offering his hand to Brenda, then Barbara. Mom motioned me forward, so I climbed into the plane on my own. Inside, Mr. Douglas directed us to seats next to small rounded windows and showed us how to use the seat belts. Then he went forward to the cockpit, sitting in the left-hand seat. Mom climbed into the plane behind us, closed the door, then walked forward, checking our seat belts again as she went.

"It will be loud in here when we start the engines," she said. "So don't worry. I'll be up front helping Mr. Douglas fly the plane."

With that, she continued forward and sat in the right-hand seat, where she buckled her seat belt and put on a radio headset just like ones we had seen in the movies. She and Mr. Douglas then started going through a printed list, flipping switches and checking dials.

Finally Mom turned to us, smiling, and said, "Here we go!"

She reached over her head to a panel of switches. Immediately, the left engine began to whine and the propeller began to slowly turn. With a loud roar and puff of smoke, the engine exploded to life. Vibrations rattled us through our seats. It was the same for the right engine. Checking dials again, Mom then spoke into her headset, and almost immediately we lurched forward.

Here we go!

Brenda was in the seat across from me, her face glued to the window, watching it all go by outside. Barbara, a bit too short to see out easily, clutched the arms of her seat and just looked around inside, a smile on her face.

We paused near the end of the runway. After a minute of final checks, Mom talked on the radio again. Then Mr. Douglas pushed two levers in the middle console forward with his right hand, while Mom held them in place with her left.

The plane rumbled forward, turning onto the runway, then accelerated, engines roaring together. Faster and faster we went as the tail began to drift back and forth. I watched Mom as she pushed the pedals with her feet and turned the wheel to keep us straight. Ten seconds later, the tail lifted off the ground, and we were level, rushing down the runway. A moment later we launched into the cool twilight air, the ground quickly dropping away from us.

We gained altitude, banking to the left in a wide arc that took us across the Missouri River and over downtown Kansas City. Tall buildings reached upward in a glowing grid of yellow-lit streets, office lights blazing. We flew past the upper floors of the tallest ones as we climbed. We could almost see into the offices as we passed.

Quickly though, we left them behind and continued south. We were flying toward an upscale shopping area in mid-town called the Country Club Plaza.

With stucco, terra-cotta, tile exterior details and tall ornate towers, the area evoked a pseudo-Spanish architecture, complete with fountains and elaborate lighting. It was touted as the first shopping center in the country. Traditionally, the merchants' association went all out with Christmas lights and decorations on the streets and buildings. From Thanksgiving to New Year's Day, nearly everyone in the city drove through the Plaza to see the lights at least one night during the season.

This year, I thought happily, we're special. We get to see them from above!

The city below spread out to the horizon. Bright streetlights along the major roads formed strings of yellow beads connecting magical puddles of light where businesses clustered at intersections. Relative darkness prevailed over the neighborhoods on either side, studded here and there with Christmas lights on houses, porch lights and widely dispersed street lights. They twinkled like stars under the bare branches of the trees as we passed overhead.

Within minutes we neared the Plaza. The plane went into a gentle banking turn, and we could see out the windows more easily.

The Plaza glowed like a fairyland, with thousands of multi-colored Christmas lights outlining every building, every tower. There were people strolling the sidewalks, peering into store windows and gathering at corners as they waited to cross the street.

Most magical of all, though, were the fountains.

The city had left the water on over the winter to keep the pipes from freezing. As a result, the graceful sculptures of rearing horses, gentle nymphs and Greek goddesses were all encrusted with a crystalline glaze of ice. In the spotlights they sparkled and glowed like brilliant diamonds, the white jets of water of the larger fountains cutting across the air in great silvery arcs.

We circled for about five minutes, then leveled out, flying southeast over the Kansas City suburbs. Mom and Mr. Douglas talked for a moment, then Mom pulled off her headset and unbuckled her seat belt. She climbed out of her seat and came back to me.

"Would you like to sit up front for a while?" she asked, smiling.

"Wow, yeah!" I nodded, eyes wide. I unbuckled and stood, then moved past her to the cockpit. Sitting down, I buckled my seat belt as I had been shown, and, at Mr. Douglas's gesture, put the headset on my head. For the next few minutes I sat in the right-hand seat, hands in my lap, as I marveled at the lights outside, at the instruments and switches inside, and at the fact that I sat at the controls of an airplane.

Mr. Douglas's voice crackled through the headset. "So Richard, do you want to fly the plane for a bit?"

"Uh, yes sir," I responded, stunned.

"All right. Now put your hands on the wheel like I'm doing, but don't push or pull on it unless I say so."

"Yes sir," I said, and raised my hands to the wheel, copying the positions of Mr. Douglas's hands.

"Okay. We're starting to gain a bit of altitude. We want to keep it at one thousand feet. That's shown by this instrument right here. So, push the wheel a bit forward, just a little. That's right. Okay, now pull it back to where it was. Good."

"Now, see this instrument? You can see it looks like a little airplane as seen from behind. Right now it's telling us that we've dropped our right wing a bit. So, turn the wheel to the left, just a little. Good, now back to the center. Yes, that's right. Just keep watching the instruments to hold our altitude and keep us level. You're doing well."

After watching me for a minute, he dropped his hands, placing them in his lap close to the wheel. "Okay Richard, you've got the airplane," he said. "That means you're the pilot."

The thought filled me with wonder. I'm flying the airplane. I'm the pilot. Mr. Douglas said so.

For a few astounding minutes, with coaching from Mr. Douglas, I flew.

Brenda's turn to sit up front came next, but she just wanted to look outside. Barbara was too young, so she stayed in back by her window with Mom. After a short while, Mr. Douglas told Brenda it was time to return to her seat, and Mom went back to the cockpit.

The flight back to the airport was all too quick, and soon we were in the car again headed home. As we laughed and chattered about what we had seen, I thought to myself: Mom flies airplanes.

Mostly guys fly airplanes, so she is special. How did she get Grampa to let her do it? I've got to ask her. She's so cool!

I want to be just like her.

Six

Rocks and Stars - 1958

"Could I have a transfer, please?" I asked the bus driver as I dropped thirty-five cents into the tall coin machine next to him. The driver ripped a thin slip of paper from a booklet and handed it to me, then without comment looked to the next passenger boarding the bus.

I turned and walked down the aisle, looking for a window seat on the right side. I liked to watch people getting on the bus and walking on the sidewalk. I didn't want to sit in back, though. It always smelled of diesel fumes from the exhaust and Grampa had sternly warned me that that's where the colored people were supposed to sit, not me.

He called them "nigras."

I was in the fifth grade now. I'd become a veteran of the Kansas City public transportation system since commuting to school on the streetcar when we lived near the railroad tracks. Things were different now, though. No more were there long afternoons in the sun looking for sparkling rocks on the tracks. Grampa had sold our little house and bought the one next door to his, so now we lived there. He had a key and would often come over on the excuse that he needed to use the phone. He was too cheap to have a line at his place. He could walk in to our home any time he wanted. We hated it.

One thing had not changed: I still ached to be a girl. I had begun cross-dressing, trying on my sister's clothes and even a few of my mother's things, whenever I dared.

A month earlier, Mom had taken us to the Kansas City Museum to see their small planetarium show and the exhibits. The Russians had recently launched their Sputnik satellite, and America was playing catch-up, trying to get its Vanguard satellite off the ground. The most recent attempt had exploded on the launching pad in front of a worldwide TV audience.

The museum was in an old mansion in the northeast part of town, part of an historic neighborhood populated by the wealthy at the turn of the century. Situated inside a low stone wall topped by a wrought-iron fence, the large, manicured property sat perched on a high bluff overlooking the Missouri River. The spacious rooms now served as exhibit spaces, and the carriage house out back had been remodeled as a planetarium.

I had enjoyed our first visit, lying back in soft seats in the dark, gazing up at the artificial stars while we listened to the volunteer talk about constellations and comets and other marvelous things. The museum itself was interesting, too, but what caught my eye was at the front counter where you bought your tickets.

In one corner of the display case, they sold mineral specimens glued to cards. Green minerals, gold minerals, all kinds. Each card had the name of the mineral, the chemical formula, and a bit about it printed on it. I badgered Mom until she relented, finally agreeing that I could go to the museum again—this time, by myself.

⨲

The bus made its slow, stop-and-go way to downtown, where I got off to wait in the heat and clouds of exhaust fumes for the second bus. There were all kinds of people at the bus stop. I even saw a man buy something in a little white envelope one time, but nobody ever bothered me.

The second bus arrived and I jumped on, handing the driver my transfer slip. After about twenty minutes, we pulled up to a stop right across the leafy green street from the museum. I crossed and ran down the long sidewalk to the huge front doors. Pulling one open, I felt cool air rush past my face. It was air-conditioned inside. I turned to the counter a few steps away.

"Hello," I said to the white-haired lady behind the counter. "Can I have a ticket for the planetarium, please?"

"That's seventy-five cents, young man," she replied, smiling. I handed over one of three crumpled dollar bills from the depths of my jeans pocket. One dollar was for bus fare home, and the last dollar and all the spare change was to buy a mineral specimen after the show. As she handed me the ticket, she said, "Better hurry. It starts in five minutes!"

I ran to the planetarium and was soon reclining in the big, soft seat, pushing it back to look up at the smooth white dome of the planetarium above me. This time the show began with a beautiful red sunset, and as it progressed we gradually saw the brighter stars, then the Milky Way, and the Moon.

Someday humans will land on the Moon, the man said.

Forty-five minutes later, I stood at the glass counter, looking at the dozen or so rocks they had for sale.

"Ma'am, could I see the green one and the shiny one? And that flat one too, please?" The nice lady unlocked the back of the display case, and pulled out the ones I wanted to see, setting them on the counter.

Picking up each one, I read the attached cards. The shiny one was iron pyrite, forming neat little gold-colored cubes all stuck together. It had come from Colorado. The flat one was muscovite mica from South Dakota, with yellowy-clear, thin transparent sheets. The green one was called aurichalcite. I'd never even heard of that one, and I knew it wasn't in my *Golden Book*. It was from Arizona. The card said it contained copper and zinc and was found near big copper deposits.

The green rock won the day. It was such a pretty color, and it had a big, long chemical formula. I handed over my dollar and change. The lady put the other rocks back in the case, then put mine in a small paper bag with a receipt. "Be careful now!" she called after me as I pushed out the door, bouncing with joy to the bus stop with my treasure.

Over the next year or two I returned to the museum several times. The nice white-haired lady was always at the counter—as if she were waiting just for me.

Seven

Schoolyard Fight - 1959

All the boys in my fifth-grade class considered girls a nuisance. They were to be avoided if possible, tolerated if not.

Not me. I preferred to spend my playground time with the girls, trading secrets and gossip, hearing about make-up and all those wonderful girl things I desperately wanted to learn. But I had to be careful.

I already knew I had to be tough. I tried to be good at kickball or running or anything boys were supposed to do. I knew that if I failed at the smallest thing, if anyone noticed that I preferred to be with the girls, it would be all over. One comment from a classmate, one little rumor and everyone would know that I was a "queer," the worst insult possible. Still, I talked to the girls as much as I dared. I knew many of them saw me as just another stupid boy, perhaps a little more curious than the rest.

However, one girl in my class was particularly nice—Patricia. She was smart and pretty. A blue-eyed blonde with a bouncy pony tail and wonderful smile, I'd had a crush on her for a long time. She was also a hot topic for the other boys. Did she "do it," they asked each other? Certainly they didn't acknowledge that none of them quite knew what "it" was.

One sunny afternoon at recess, after being picked nearly last for the kickball team, I waited for my turn at the plate. The girls had gathered by the playground fence, sitting and talking among themselves. I inched over to hear what they were saying.

Patricia spotted me. "Come sit down," she called out.

With a big smile on my face, I said "Thanks!" and quickly sat with them. Just a few minutes, I told myself. Just a few....

Soon we were chatting away, having a wonderful time. Suddenly there was a commotion in the background, laughter and shouting. The boys had stopped their game, snickering at me surrounded by the girls. It was my turn to kick.

"Look at the little girlie," one of them shouted.

It was Roy Lundville, the bully and gang leader of the class.

"Maybe we can find a nice pretty dress for you to play in," he continued, grinning. My face turned bright red with embarrassment. I looked at the girls as I stood.

"I have to go now."

Patricia, looking back at Roy with an imperious air, spoke up in a loud, haughty voice, "Don't let them pick on you Richard. You're nice, and they are definitely not!"

"Thanks," I said.

My stomach churning, I walked over to the plate to take my turn. At that moment a teacher stepped out of the building and blew her whistle. Recess was over. As we filed back into the school building, Roy came up behind me and gave me a shove. "I'll be seeing you after school, little girlie," he smirked.

It was difficult to focus in class that afternoon, as I dreaded the looming confrontation. But worst of all, my desire to play with the girls rather than the boys was now public knowledge.

I shouldn't have done it. I am marked forever, I thought. Now I am that "queer" everyone can see, can laugh at, can make fun of. and pick on.

Three-fifteen. The bell rang. I made my way down the noisy hallway full of students escaping their classrooms toward the heavy doors leading out of the building, dreading going outside.

As I exited I found myself surrounded by a waiting crowd. There were more kids waiting with Roy in a grassy area near the school's flagpole.

"C'mere, little girlie," taunted Roy as I tried to slip through the crowd. "Wanna play house?"

No escape.

Resigning myself, I trudged over to the flagpole as the taunts and jeers filled my ears. I dropped my books to the ground near the flagpole, then turned to move toward him, my heart racing. Roy, big for his age, was accompanied by his usual gang, all trying to act tough and grinning in anticipation of the beating to come. My mind spinning, I tried to think of a way out.

But there was no way I could avoid this fight. It was going to happen no matter what, and I realized in that moment that I must never, ever give in. I had to make it so no one would ever pick on me again. I had to prove that I was a real boy and not a queer and that I could defend myself.

I stood for a moment, considering what to do.

Okay, I thought, Roy is big, but maybe he is slow. If I move fast enough and surprise him, I might have a chance.

Looking down at the ground, I approached. When just a few feet from him, I quickly lowered my head and ran toward him with all my strength. He didn't react in time, and I hit him in the stomach. I felt his soft belly give way, his belt buckle scratching my nose. Still driving forward, I grabbed at his legs, trying to pull his feet out from under him. Partly successful, we both toppled to the ground in a tangled, squirming heap. Kids were yelling and screaming, but I barely heard them.

We fought for control. Quickly, it became apparent he was stronger than me. Roy got a hold on my right arm by the wrist, and pushed it back. At the same time, he rolled out from under me. Almost immediately we were on our sides, both scrambling to get high enough to sit on top of the other.

Roy won.

He managed to get his feet under him and drove forward, slamming me on my back against the dirt. He jumped, swinging his leg over and straddling me across my chest, grabbing at my arms.

At that moment, the school's vice principal, Mr. Armour, reached the edge of the crowd. It parted like water before him.

"You two!" he bellowed angrily. "Come with me immediately!" He scanned the mob of suddenly quiet children. "The rest of you—go home!" He turned on his heel and marched away to his office in the school building. Roy and I stood up, dusted ourselves off without a word and followed him.

Mr. Armour entered his office and took the seat behind his huge oak desk, hands steepled. When I entered, he silently pointed, indicating that I was to remain standing on the left. When Roy arrived, he was told to stand on the right.

"I don't know what started this fight, and I don't care," Mr. Armour declared. "You are both hereby suspended from school for three days. I will be calling your mother, Mr. Shepard, and your parents, Mr. Lundville, to discuss the matter."

He looked at me with a disapproving stare and asked, "Mr. Shepard, are you hurt?" I shook my head no. "And you, Mr. Lundville?"

"No, sir."

Mr. Armour turned back to me. "Mr. Shepard, get out of my office. Go directly home. Is that clear?"

"Yes sir."

"Mr. Lundville, you will wait in the hallway until I tell you to leave. Understood?"

"Yes sir."

I turned and left the room, slowly walking down the empty hall. Outside, my books were still on the ground. The girls stood around them, including Patricia. As I got closer, she looked at me with concern. "Are you okay?" she asked.

"Yeah," I replied. "I'm okay."

After a pause, Patricia asked, "Why did you fight him?"

"I had to. I had to show that I could defend myself," I said. "And I wanted to make him leave me alone from now on."

"Too bad," she responded.

She gazed at me for a moment, sadness in her eyes, then turned away. The other girls followed, leaving me standing there.

I stared after them. I felt stupid and embarrassed. I had only done what was expected of me, the "manly" thing, but I had lost their friendship because of it.

I had accomplished nothing. I had revealed my perverted, queer soul for all to see. Inside me there was only a nasty, bitter taste of embarrassment and lost friendships.

What else could I do? I thought. I had to fight back. I'm supposed to fight back, right?

But worst of all was knowing—knowing that they were right about me. In secret, I still tried on my mother's and sisters' clothes at home.

I knew if I were exposed, I'd be destroyed. They'd send me to the loony bin, the state mental hospital, where they did things to people with electricity and chemicals and pills—people like me. If I were lucky maybe they'd just put me in a cold, empty room for months at a time and feed me drugs to "fix" me.

No, I had to fight back—or else.

Eight

Besame Red - 1963

Yet I could not stop.

Through grade school and now as a high school freshman, I took every opportunity to secretly try on women's clothes: my sisters' and my mother's. I tried various things to see if they fit or how they looked in the mirror. I became good at memorizing the positions and placements of the clothes I tried on, putting them back exactly without anyone being the wiser.

In my daily life, I was just as careful. The way I used my hands when I talked, the tilt of my head, the timbre of my voice, my choice of words—any number of habits or mannerisms became potential clues revealing my feminine side. I suppressed them, squeezed them into oblivion, trying to banish them from my very existence.

On weekdays, Mom always worked till five, and my younger sisters often went to their girlfriends' houses after school to play. After all, who wanted to play with a "dumb boy," especially if he was your older brother?

So, when I was home alone, I dressed up. Being cautious, I tried only a pair of shoes or perhaps a skirt at first, daring to take off my jeans. But as time wore on, I became bolder.

41

One sunny Friday afternoon, a rare opportunity presented itself. My sisters had gone to a friend's house for dinner. Mom wouldn't get home from work for at least two hours.

It was time enough.

As I searched through Mom's closet, I found a new box I hadn't seen before. To my utter delight it contained a burgundy-colored shirtdress. The sheen of the soft, richly-colored fabric was almost metallic in the sunlight streaming through the window. Wonder of wonders, the dress nearly fit me. With the dress were two petticoats, the lacy kind that made your skirt stand out from your body. With these treasures and this much time, I can go all out, I thought excitedly.

I pulled out a pair of Mom's stockings and garter belt from her chest of drawers, and also retrieved a pair of high heels that I knew I could squeeze my feet into. To complete the look, I stuffed one of her bras with socks. I put each item on slowly, then the petticoats, and finally, carefully, the dress. With heart pounding, I tottered on the high heels over to my mother's dresser.

I had never before had the courage to try make-up, always worried that I would not be able to cover my tracks. Mom would surely notice the disturbed powder or lipstick.

But I couldn't let the moment pass. I just couldn't.

Mascara first. Carefully, I pulled the little brush out of its slender tube, and stroked it onto my eyelashes, followed by streaks of eye shadow, darkening my upper lids. I tied a scarf around my head babushka style, trying to make it look as feminine as possible. I clipped on a pair of earrings from my mother's collection. Finally, I dabbed liquid foundation on my finger and smeared it on my nose and cheeks, trying to spread it evenly. Then I looked in the mirror.

It was almost comical. I looked like I'd gotten poison ivy on my face and had to cover it in calamine lotion. I'd also smudged mascara under one eye in my clumsiness.

I didn't care.

My hands shaking, I picked up a tube of Mom's lipstick. On the bottom was written the color—Besame Red. Moving closer to the mirror, I slowly, carefully applied it, following my upper lip line, then the lower, being sure to cover the back of my lips well. When I finished, I dabbed my lips with a piece of toilet paper as I had seen Mom do. Done, I stepped back from the mirror to see the overall results.

Despite my clownish efforts with the make-up, the ill-fitting dress and absurd petticoats, as disturbing as I would have looked to another person, I saw something else entirely.

I saw a girl. She was there, inside me, looking out from behind my eyes.

For the first time, I saw past my boyish, acned face, my bony pointed Adam's apple. I saw a girl.

This is wonderful, I thought.

What if I had been born a girl? I'd be Mom's oldest daughter. What a delicious word, daughter! Mom would teach me about clothes and makeup. My sisters wouldn't hate me, we'd play together and share clothes. We'd talk about the icky boys at school and what we wanted to do when we grew up. I wouldn't be so alone any more.

No, this is terrible, I screamed in my mind. Absolutely terrible.

I am a boy, a stinking, stupid boy. And I'm standing here wearing a dress and earrings and Mom's makeup. Why is that? I might as well be dead.

Tears welled up in my eyes, which I tried to wipe away. It only caused the mascara to run. That stings, I noted through the tears. But I continued to stand in front of the mirror, ashamed at the image before me, but fascinated as well.

What am I?

The sound of a key being inserted in the front door lock cut through the silence. In a heart-racing panic I dashed out of Mom's bedroom, sprinting down the hall. I just made it to my bedroom door when I glanced down the stairwell, only to see my mother staring up at me, her mouth open in shock.

I dove inside, shutting the door behind me.

Hurriedly, I ripped off the clothes, stashing them around the room wherever I could hide them. Then I slipped out of my room and tiptoed to the bathroom, where I proceeded to scrub my face, hard, concentrating on my lips and around my eyes, trying to remove any trace of makeup. As I dried my face, I knew that I must go downstairs and face my mother sooner or later.

Heart in my mouth, I shuffled down and around the corner into the kitchen.

"Hi Mom," I said.

"Hi Richard, how was your day?" Mom replied.

With an internal sigh of relief I thought, maybe I got away with it? No, that couldn't be. She saw me, I know she did. What's she going to do?

But nothing was said until a week later. As I helped her with the dinner dishes one evening she turned and looked me in the eye. "Did you like it?" she asked softly.

I knew immediately what she meant.

"Oh, no," I quickly responded. "I was just bored and messing around. I'm sorry."

"Oh."

She turned away, but I saw her worried look.

It was never mentioned again.

In the weeks that followed, guilt gnawed at me. I had been doing this for so long, this terrible, perverted thing—sneaking into closets, posing in front of mirrors. Yet that was only the surface manifestation of my crime.

Most damning of all—more than anything else—was the silent, aching desire in my soul—to be a girl.

TRANS-FORMATIONS

Nine

The Library - 1964

"Mom told me so," Brenda said, a sly smile on her face. "You were born with your gonads stuck up inside you. They had to dig them out."

"That's a lie!" I yelled back. "You're lying, she never told me that! You take it back!"

"I am not! You just ask her!" she retorted, then turned and marched to her room, slamming the door behind her.

I stood in the hallway, dumbfounded. Oh my god, I thought, is that why I want to be a girl? Was I supposed to be a girl when I was born? Do they know I have been trying on their clothes? Do Brenda and Barbara talk about me behind my back to their friends, to everyone?

I didn't know what to think. Fifteen now, I knew I liked girls. I was attracted to them, I wanted to be around them, wanted to experience all the things a horny, inexperienced teenager dreamed about. Kissing. Making out. Sex.

Yet I was faced with the terrible conundrum of wanting to be a girl at the same time. I wanted to be kissed, to make out and have sex—but as the girl. By now, I'd masturbated many times. Yet I did not fantasize about making love to a girl. Instead, in my fantasy, I was the girl being made love to, somehow the object of someone's affections.

Yet I wasn't sexually attracted to men. In those fantasies I saw myself with a vague, shapeless person, an entity of pure imagination. I dreamed of one who would gently satisfy my needs, anticipate my desires. Most importantly, it would be a person who loved me, who wouldn't care if I wore a flowery summer dress or dirty jeans, wouldn't care if I loved cars or music or art. A being who would see me for my true self and yet, after all that, still love me. Love me, despite it all, perhaps even because of it all.

But the voice in my head knew better.

I walked into my bedroom and shut the door. Sitting at my small desk by the window, I stared out into the bleak winter sky.

If it's true about my body, what Brenda said, is that the reason I want to be a girl? Or is it because Dad left us? Maybe deep down I think that if I'm a girl he will love me and come back?

No, that's just plain stupid, the voice whispered. He's never coming back, he wants nothing to do with a fucking sissy. Give it up, quit looking for excuses.

Quit crying like a little girl, dammit.

I filed onto the bus with the other passengers, dropping three quarters into the tall machine next to the driver and moving toward a vacant window seat on the right side a few aisles back. It was a Saturday, so the bus wasn't full.

Ever since Mom caught me and Brenda taunted me, I desperately wanted to find more information about my "problem," this perverted longing that inhabited my soul.

In the last few years, I had heard the words: words like her-
maphrodite, transvestite, cross-dresser, drag queen. Might I be one
of them? I'd heard of Christine Jorgenson years ago, but never had
the courage to seek out her book. Someone might have seen me
with it, or Mom would find it.

But now, now I needed to know.

Is there is a cure? Will it go away as I get older? Would it fade
away if I got married? I had no answers to questions I dared not
ask. I had to find out for myself.

I had visited the local branch library, but the few psychology
books there had offered no insights. I needed to find more technical and thorough texts. So, on the pretense of doing research for
an English paper, I decided to make a trip to the main library in
downtown Kansas City. Perhaps, hidden amidst the larger collection, was an answer.

I stepped off the bus and walked two blocks to the Kansas
City Public Library, the main building for the entire system, and
the library with the largest general book collection in the metro-
politan area.

A new building, the library stood four stories tall—a block of
aluminum, glass and flat blue panels with a large, open foyer on
the first floor. I passed through the revolving doors into the cool,
open space, walking over to the area that held the card catalog.

Moving along the bank of wooden drawers, I scanned the
tags on the fronts for the spelling "Psych." Finding the drawer and
sifting through the cards, it appeared that most of the psychology
books were clustered in one section of the library on the second
floor. I wrote down the Dewey decimal code number and trudged
upstairs to see what I might find.

The second floor was quiet. A few people, mostly college-age students, were scattered around tables as they worked. My plodding footsteps intruded on the relative quiet around me, so, stepping as quietly as I could, I walked along the tall shelves, scanning the numbers posted on the ends.

Near the end of the row I found the psychology section.

Checking furtively to see if anyone was watching, I disappeared between the shelves and began searching titles in the wall of books. Soon I found the psychology textbooks. I opened some at random, looking in the table of contents and index for anything to do with cross-dressing or transvestites.

I found nothing at first, and it seemed that there would be no help here. But as I moved down the shelves, I came to the Abnormal Psychology section.

Yeah, that's me, I thought.

I leafed through the heavy texts one by one. Suddenly, I held in my sweaty hand a book with the word in the index: *Transvestism.* Hurriedly I thumbed through to find the page.

The reference was a single paragraph tacked on to the end of a chapter on perversion and fetishism. The final sentence screamed at me from the page:

"Transvestites are little more than fetishistic narcissists
who want to have their cake and eat it too."

I stood, dumbfounded, faintly dizzy, ears ringing. I had hoped, even prayed for some glimmer of understanding and hope. Instead, I stood in the abnormal psychology section, reading about myself—me, a pervert, a queer, a "fetishistic narcissist." No glimmer of a cure, no path to redemption.

The author has a Ph.D. and has written a book, I thought. He must know.

I slid the book back into its slot, and almost staggered to the nearest table, dropping into a chair. Staring out the window at the empty sky, I considered my options.

If I tell Mom, or anyone about myself they'll put me away. They'll lock me up and use drugs or electric shock or something worse to "fix" me.

If someone finds out, if someone catches me again, I'd just have to kill myself. Maybe that's it. Maybe I should just kill myself before I'm caught again. I would save myself this pain and Mom the embarrassment of discovering I'm a pervert.

Yet I don't want to die. I just want to be a girl. Was I supposed to be a girl when I was born? Is there a girl inside me, or am I just crazy?

So. There it is. No one is going to help me, and I don't want to die.

Okay. That means the only option I have is to make this go away. From now on, I won't dress up. I'll be a man. I'll just stop.

I am not going to be a pervert any more.

TRANS-FORMATIONS

Ten

Elmer -1965

"I'll have the chicken burrito, please," I said, looking up at the cute waitress. I watched as she walked away to turn in our order, wondering what it must be like to be her. She was pretty and confident. She knew I was watching.

Mom and I were having dinner out, something we did from time to time as I got older. As the years without Dad went by, she and I became close in the face of Grampa's overbearing control and the turmoil of our lives. Now sixteen, I was trying to be what I was expected to be, the dutiful son, the "man of the house." My sisters, Brenda and Barbara, felt the dysfunction worse than I did.

It wasn't Mom's fault, I knew. She had to work for the food on our table, for the clothes on our backs. She had no options. But that left us either in Grampa's clutches or on our own.

I turned my head back from the waitress to see Mom looking at me. She waited for a moment, then said, "Richard, I'd like to ask you something. It's something I've been thinking about for a while, and I'm not committed to it yet, but I want your feelings on the matter."

"Okay," I said. "What's wrong?"

"Oh, nothing's wrong," she replied, smiling. "What it is, well, is Elmer. He's asked me to marry him."

Elmer was Betty's dad. Betty was our occasional babysitter. We had known her and Elmer for perhaps two years, and had even gone to their house for Thanksgiving, where we met his wife Doris and his son Bill. Doris was nice but in poor health. A few months after that dinner, she passed away.

A pipe fitter by trade, Elmer was a short, fat, bald man with strong hairy arms and a round belly. He liked his beer. He had been nice to us kids, and there was almost a "Santa Claus" feel about him. But it also felt odd when he spoke to us. He rarely looked us in the eye or talked to us as individual people. We were just "the kids" to Elmer.

"Umm, okay," I replied. "Do you love him?"

"I think so," she said, a little uncertain. "He's nice to be around, he treats me well, and I enjoy his company. He's got a good job and can take good care of us. I'm just worried that you and the girls might not like the idea, so I'm talking to each of you first."

"Is that enough, that he is nice and has a good job?" I asked, worried that my question was in some way antagonistic. Why would Mom be attracted to Elmer?

"Well Richard, it's like this: I'm lonely. Can you understand that?"

I nodded. I understood loneliness very well.

"I'm also hoping that Elmer can be a good influence. He can provide a male role model for you and the girls and stability that we haven't had in our lives. I don't mean to offend you, but he's commented that you seem a bit "effeminate" to him. Anyway, I'd like to hear how you feel about the idea."

I pondered for a moment, looking at her. Effeminate, I thought? Sorry, Mom, but you have no idea.

But I was worried for her. She's lonely, she said, and all of us were unhappy under Grampa's yoke. I couldn't really be the "man of the house," no matter how hard I tried, and certainly couldn't be the companion she wanted. So, Elmer will be okay, I decided. I just hope I can continue to dress when I need to.

"It's okay by me, Mom," I said. "Just so you're happy."

"Thank you, Richard," she replied, smiling. "I'll talk to your sisters tomorrow, so don't mention it to them, please."

We drove home, chatting about how things would work. Elmer would move into our house, she said.

As we turned into our driveway, Grampa suddenly emerged from his front door and marched over to us. He had clearly been waiting for us to get home.

"Margaret, I'd like to speak to you," he said seriously, standing next to the driver's-side door.

"Okay, what's the problem?" Mom replied as she turned off the engine.

Grampa hesitated, looking uncomfortably at me in the passenger seat. He made his decision, then began speaking.

"I don't think this marriage to Mr. Thompson is a good idea. I don't believe he is the right man for you. He's not well educated, and he doesn't come from a good background, as far as I can tell. I will give you two hundred fifty dollars to call it off."

Silence. I stared at Grampa, my mouth hanging open. Grampa had just offered Mom money to give up her happiness.

Mom paused for a long moment, then looked him straight in the eye.

"No," she said.

She started the car, put it in gear, and drove down the driveway to the back of the house, saying nothing as tears leaked out of her hurt and angry eyes.

The first few weeks were okay. Elmer was nice to Mom, and tolerated us kids. Then, one evening at dinner, things began to change.

"There'll be no talking at the dinner table. You're here to eat, not chatter like a bunch of idiots. Keep it quiet."

I looked from Elmer to Mom. She looked as surprised as we were, but said nothing. We finished our meal in silence. After she finished washing the dishes, Mom slipped up to her room while Elmer lumbered to the basement. Down there, he had set up a desk where he fashioned his own fishing lures. He remained there in the semi-darkness for hours, lit only by the lamp over the desk, making lures and drinking beer.

Santa Claus had a dark side, it appeared.

I went upstairs and knocked on Mom's door.

"Come in," she said.

"Hi Mom. You okay?" I asked.

"Yes, I'm fine," she replied. She was reading a book. There was a tall orange-colored drink on the bedside table. A screwdriver.

"Mom, why do we have to be quiet at dinner? It's the only time we ever talk to each other, 'cause we're all home."

"Well, Richard, he's the man of the house now, and he has the right to make some of the rules. He likes it quiet at dinner, so I think we can give it a try for a while. He's just learning how we work as a family and is trying to figure things out. Let's give him a break. He needs to feel accepted, don't you think?"

"I guess so," I replied uncertainly.

"Now, don't you have some homework to do?"

"Yeah."

I went to my room down the short hall, still troubled.

Is this what it's like in a real family, I wondered? Grampa is kinda that way, too. Are Elmer and Grampa just being manly? I don't understand it. They make us feel like we don't matter, that what we want or how we feel is stupid. Why do men have to control things all the time?

One thing was clear, though—I was not the man of the house anymore.

"Dammit, just put the minnow on the hook the way I showed you!" Elmer snarled.

Two months after he announced his rule for silence at dinner, he took me fishing. The trip developed into an aching, bitter weekend for me, sleeping elbow-to-elbow in a pickup truck camper with a fat, angry man I had quickly learned to hate. It was a weekend during which I could do nothing right, and every word I spoke was stupid. Eventually, I just stopped talking, as I fervently wished the earth would swallow me up and get it over with. The silence between us was punctured only by the occasional necessity of communication or his need to criticize me. It was a battlefield, a test of his need to dominate and my will to endure.

Sorry, little fish, I said to myself, and plunged the hook through its belly and out the back. Hooked this way, the minnow wiggled, attracting larger fish. I tossed the whole mess into the river, and sat down on a rock to wait.

So, this is fishing, I mused. I guess it'd be okay if I could drink beer.

After about ten minutes of staring at the thick, brown water as it oozed by, the little red and white bobber suddenly dunked below the surface.

"You've got a nibble," Elmer hissed, "Now hook him!"

As instructed, I carefully picked up the pole, and with one swift motion whipped it upward in a wide arc. It felt like there was an old tire on the end of the line as the tip of the pole bent downward. I pulled up again, this time reeling in a bit of line. Then again. After three pulls the bobber came out of the water, followed by a big, fat glistening fish. It wasn't fighting.

"You finally caught a fish!" Elmer exclaimed as he lifted it out of the water.

"What kind is it?"

It looked like it was in pain, curled up like that.

"Oh, it's just a carp," he replied. "Maybe three pounds. Not much use and no good to eat. Just take it off the hook and throw it back in. Here, use the long-nose pliers to get the hook out so you don't stab yourself."

Glad I didn't have to stick my fingers into the fish's mouth, I twisted the pliers to pull out the hook, then threw the fish into the murky water, where it disappeared.

Thankfully, the minnow was still on the hook. I didn't have to eviscerate yet another poor creature. I swung my pole, propelling my hook and sad minnow back into the river, fervently hoping I wouldn't get another bite.

My luck held. I got no bites for the rest of the day. Elmer caught a big bass which he quickly gutted, expertly using his thin filet knife to slit its belly and pull out the innards with his hand.

As he did it I was thinking, he could do that to me if he wanted. He probably would if he knew I was a pervert.

When he finished, we had two pieces for our dinner. He threw the remains back into the river. He fried the fish over the campfire that evening in a little oil with salt and pepper, along with some canned beans. We ate in silence. He drank a couple more beers, while I sipped an orange soda. The fish was bony, but good.

The best part, though, was that we were going home tomorrow morning.

The tension between Elmer and me worsened over the ensuing months, as he exerted more and more control over all of us. The nice round man we knew before the marriage had, in the space of a few months, transformed into a self-centered, bloated child. I came to hate him for what he was, for what he was doing to us. We weren't a family as we had so wistfully hoped. Instead, we were prisoners.

"Don't try to confront him, Richard. He's strong and might hurt you."

Mom's warning made me pause, knowing full well she was right. Even if I did win some kind of confrontation, it would be a foolish victory. I still had to live in the house, and he'd never leave simply because my sisters and I didn't like him. He'd just bear down harder on us, and Mom would be the one to suffer. Once again, Mom was caught in the middle.

"Okay, Mom," I said. "I'll just try to keep out of his way."

"Thank you, that'd be best, I think," she said. "And Richard, I wanted to talk to you about something else."

"Okay," I said slowly, worried.

"You turned seventeen last week, and you're almost finished with your junior year in high school. Have you thought about what you are going to do after you graduate?"

"Not really," I confessed. "I guess I could go to college here in town, but my grades aren't all that great. Maybe find a job?"

"Well, that's not much of a plan," she said. "Especially considering the draft and what is going on in Vietnam. I have a suggestion. One of the men at work is a retired Marine Major. He told me about a program with the Naval Air Reserve where you can finish high school and then pick the specialty training you want. It's just outside of town at the Naval Air Station in Olathe, Kansas. Would you be willing to go and talk with them?"

I pondered the idea for a moment. Not the regular Navy, but the Air Reserves. Maybe the Navy would teach me to fly? Even better, I could escape Elmer before we kill each other. There's the war, though. Would I have to go? Mom thinks it's a good idea. And I'd get the GI Bill to help out with school expenses. Of course, there's my little problem. Would it go away? Could I hide it?

"If you say so," I replied, uncertain.

"Good. We'll go down there this weekend and see what it's all about."

The following Saturday morning we drove to the air station. By two o'clock that dizzying afternoon, Mom had signed the papers. I found myself enlisted in the Naval Air Reserves. It was May 23rd, 1965, and in two weeks I would start boot camp.

PART TWO

Sedimentary

In time, the swirling magma with its swarms of mineral crystals will find its way to the surface. The resulting volcanic eruption may be relatively benign, or it may be catastrophic. Nevertheless, the fragile crystals are thrown from their womb out into the world, alighting wherever the vagaries of wind and chance deposit them. There, entirely different forces and processes come into play as their journey into the wider world begins.

We too leave home to make our way in the world. Our departure may be bitter or sweet, early or late, but it must happen if we are to continue to grow. We step into the unpredictable world and learn to adapt as best we can.

TRANS-FORMATIONS

Eleven

Boot Camp - 1965

"Platoon, Ten-Hut!" bawled the drill instructor.

Sixty-three of us "Boots" snapped to attention, facing the bright Kansas sunrise. We stood as we had been trained, heels together, feet at forty-five degree angles, thumbs on the seams of our dungarees, and eyes straight ahead. Bosun's Mate First Class Jones was no one to mess with, so you'd damned well better do it right or many pushups would ensue. It had been four long, rigorous weeks under his tender care. There were eight more to go.

"Awright, listen up," he continued. "We have the results of last week's tests. When you hear your name called, sing out."

"Reynolds!"

"SIR, YES SIR!" came the loud response.

"You came in first. Shepard!"

"SIR, YES SIR!"

"You came in second. Rodrigo!"

"SIR, YES SIR!"

"You came in third. You three are released from fire watch and K.P. duty for next week. Well done."

"Awright, Platoons – right face! Forwaard, harch!"

As we marched off to class, I was thrilled. I came in second! Out of all the guys in the platoon, I came in second! Maybe I'm not so stupid after all?

In our classes, we were being indoctrinated into the rigors of the Uniform Code of Military Justice, routines of shipboard operations, and aircraft operations aboard aircraft carriers, as well as all the minutiae and discipline of being in the Navy. All the while, we marched and swam and breathed tear gas and jogged around the base and polished our boots and washed our clothes in buckets and marched some more. We also cleaned the barracks and marched and polished a big transport airplane and our boots and marched even more.

I succeeded in all of it, to my surprise.

"So Will, how do you get your boots so shiny?"

Half a dozen of us were gathered around the table in our barracks, polishing our work shoes, called "boondockers," for tomorrow's inspection. Will had been called out for the excellent shine on his more than once in the last weeks, and now he was revealing his secret.

"Well, a couple of things," he replied. "First, use the Kiwi wax, not that other stuff. It's softer and goes on smoother. Second, I use panty hose."

"Huh? Panty hose?"

"Yeah," he said, smiling. He pulled a pair of dirty-looking hose out of his boot bag.

"Here's the deal. After you put a layer of wax on the toe of the boot, you use the panty hose to buff the wax so it's even all across

66

the toe. It works kinda like real fine-grained sandpaper on wood. Then finish using a t-shirt and spit. The final step is to warm up the wax with flame from a cigarette lighter. Not too much; just enough to re-melt it to a glaze. Let it cool, and there ya go!"

Now our platoon wouldn't continue to get "gigged" for poorly shined boondockers. For me, however, it meant something else entirely. I now had an excuse to carry panty hose in my sea bag.

I almost regretted the thought. Almost.

"They've been posted!" came the yell from the barracks hallway.

The final grades for the long twelve weeks of Boot Camp were pinned to the big bulletin board, where before, duty rosters had determined our daily fate and patriotic Navy posters hung depicting heroic ships at sea, with fighter aircraft streaking overhead. We rushed out to see the final standings.

Today was our last day. After the graduation ceremony this afternoon, many of us newly minted young sailors would travel to permanent duty stations at naval air bases on land or to ships for duty at sea. A few others, like me, were to be released to the Reserves to finish out high school, after which we each would go on to a Navy specialty school, an "A" School as they were called. I had qualified to be an Aerographer's Mate, better known in the Navy as a "weather guesser."

Crowding with the others around the board, I made my way forward to see the list. I had come in fourth, out of sixty-three of my fellow Boots. Fourth.

I looked to see who had come in third, and saw that I had missed third place by half a point.

I had done well. I had adapted and learned not only about the Navy, but I had also learned an important lesson, perhaps the most important one of my life. I learned that if I applied myself, I could succeed.

I had never before felt I did anything well. It was a revelation.

Twelve

USS Kitty Hawk - 1967

"Goodbye, Mom."

I could barely hold back my tears as we stood at the gate in the Kansas City Municipal Airport—the same airport we had flown from that wonderful Christmas so long ago.

I had been ordered to join the aircraft carrier Kitty Hawk in San Diego to begin my active duty in the Navy. According to our agreement, I owed them two years.

"You be careful," Mom said, her eyes glistening and solemn. She was sending her only son off to war.

"Thanks, Mom, I will."

I thanked her for encouraging me to join the Naval Air Reserve, which saved me from the draft and almost certain combat. "Thanks to you, nobody is going to be shooting at me." I hugged her hard for a long moment, then turned to board the plane, not looking back. I knew that if I looked back, I'd cry.

I traveled in my Navy dress blues, my new rank carefully sewn on the left arm showing a white eagle above a single red chevron signifying Petty Officer Third Class. Wearing the uniform was a requirement for getting the cheap plane ticket offered to active duty servicemen. Of course, that meant everyone saw I was in the military and that I was headed off to the war.

For some, this was an honorable thing. I was doing my patriotic duty for my country. For others, it made me an ignorant warmonger rushing headlong to Vietnam to murder and oppress the poor blameless villagers.

Me? I just wanted to get out alive and move on with my life.

By early evening I stood on the pier at Naval Base San Diego. Above me loomed the astounding gray bulk of the Kitty Hawk.

Her gray steel hulk stood six stories tall at the flight deck and another four stories higher on what's called "the island." Brightly lit by spotlights and internal lighting, she smelled of diesel fuel and sea water. The rumble of machinery reverberated through my feet, even on the dock. The shipboard announcements echoed over the P.A. system. More than five thousand sailors lived on this behemoth.

It seemed surreal, a bad dream somehow, going to war. Locked up on this floating prison with thousands of guys for months on end, would someone spot me? Would I be able to pull off my "real man" act? Living in such close quarters, someone might notice a wayward feminine gesture, a soft attitude or way of speaking. No, I drink my coffee black, thanks, I'd say. No sissies here.

The risks of war were one thing, but getting caught would be quite another. They beat people like me. Sometimes worse.

No one would care about one less queer in the world.

Taking a deep breath, I slung my heavy olive-drab sea bag to my shoulder and stepped up to the gangway, leaving behind the world I knew. "Permission to come aboard, sir," I said, as I saluted first the unseen flag at the stern of the ship, then Officer of the Deck at the top of the gangway, just as I had been taught. He saluted back.

"Permission granted," he replied. "Got your orders?"

I handed him the manila envelope containing the all-important paperwork of my Navy existence. Pulling them out, he took a quick look.

"Ah, so you're a new weather guesser. Okay, just stand by over there. I'll have the duty seaman take you to your quarters."

He turned to the next man who had come up the gangplank behind me. He carried a sea bag as well.

Ten minutes and a series of stairs and passageways later, I stood at the compartment door. I paused a moment, then pulled aside the curtain and stepped over the sill into the dimly lit space.

The compartment was a square space perhaps fifteen feet per side. To the left and in front of me, bunk beds were stacked three high and close together. Each bunk had a curtain on a wire stretched across its length.

Against the wall to the right stood a card table. Faint music trickled from the speakers of a television mounted on the wall over my right shoulder. Overhead were thick wires and pipes interlaced in bundles, interspersed by a few fluorescent light fixtures.

Two young sailors sat at the table, playing cards. As I stepped in, they looked up.

"Hey there," one said. "You must be the new guy."

"Yeah," I said, extending my hand. "My name's Rick."

"I'm Ron and this is Daniel. Welcome to the Shitty Kitty," they said as we shook hands.

"So, how many guys are in the division?" I asked.

"There's twenty-two of us living in this compartment, then the Chief and our Commanding Officer have their own quarters, so twenty-four in total. Since we're in port, a lot of the guys are on leave or out on liberty right now. You'll get to know them soon enough."

"Have you checked in at the office yet?" Ron asked.

"No, they brought me here first."

"Okay, just drop your sea bag, and I'll take you over to the office to check in with the Chief. Our office is on the other side of the ship, under the island."

✍

"Welcome to the Division," Chief Higgins said.

The Chief was a short, dark-haired man with a pockmarked face and a hard glint in his watery blue eyes. Was that a sense of humor, I wondered, or the look of a shark spying a lone fish?

"So, how did you do in 'A' School?" he asked.

"I came in third out of a class of thirty-five, Chief," I replied.

"Why didn't you come in first?" he quickly responded, a sharp smile on his face.

"Uhh, beer, Chief."

He laughed, throwing his head back. "Yeah, that'd do it! I see from your record that you just turned eighteen, didn't you, and you found out they'd let you into the Enlisted Men's Club on base, right?"

"Yes, I'm afraid so," I said, looking down at my feet.

"No problem, Mister Shepard. I appreciate your honesty," he said, still smiling.

"Okay, let's talk about your job. You are going to handle the Strike Weather reports."

The Chief went on to explain. I was to listen for weather reports from pilots operating over the target areas, plot them on a small map board, then post the map in the Operations Center. The Chief showed me my desk and the speaker on the wall tuned to the radio frequency used by the aircraft.

Turning back he said, "When we're at sea we work Port and Starboard watches. That's twelve hours on duty, twelve hours off, seven days a week. When we're in port it's an eight-to-five job, unless you've got the overnight duty. There's always at least one person on duty at all times.

"I'll get one of the guys who's done the job to show you the ropes tomorrow. Today, just get settled in. Get to know the ship. I'll see you for the morning watch. Any questions?"

"No, I don't think so, Chief. Thanks."

At sea three months later, much more than code numbers came over the strike radio frequency. It was January 30th, 1968, the start of the Tet Offensive.

As part of a three-carrier strike group positioned in the Gulf of Tonkin, Vietnam, we cruised around a spot in the middle of the ocean designated Yankee Station. That made us prominent members of the "Gulf of Tonkin Yacht Club."

Aircraft operating off the Kitty Hawk included F-4 Phantoms, A-4 Skyhawks, A-6 Intruders and half a dozen other craft. In South Vietnam below the DMZ, they supported troops on the ground. In the North, they attacked the infrastructure of the country in an attempt to limit North Vietnam's ability to carry out the war.

It wasn't working very well.

Listening for weather reports, I occasionally heard plane-to-plane chatter. Once, in the middle of a report from an F-4 Phantom, the pilot yelled, "They're throwing telephone poles at us!" His transmission broke off. I never knew if he was hit by the surface-to-air missiles or just changed frequencies.

That's how we experienced the war aboard ship—as a distant rumble somewhere over the horizon. Planes sometimes returned with damage; others didn't return at all. We never knew how things were going. We were just part of the machinery, cogs in the elaborate war machine that was a Navy task force at sea.

We received regular news reports on the internal television system, produced right on the ship. The reports were so censored and slanted, they were laughable. We were told that we were making great strides for democracy in Southeast Asia, winning hearts and minds, taking the fight to the dirty little enemy in black pajamas. Of course, back home all good Americans supported the war as a necessary defense of freedom and the United States of America. Mom and apple pie survived because of what we were doing for our country. Hippies and protestors? They caused only minor disturbances. They were all faggots and drug addicts anyway.

The lies were obvious. Yet we were a captive audience, locked in our metal shell, fed the company line and expected to salute it at every turn, or else.

But I was curious. For a few days, whenever I went to the mess hall for chow, I asked whichever guy sat across from me why he thought we were there, and why he was there.

A few spouted the party line, some even going so far as to say, "My country, right or wrong." Those were mostly "lifers," bent on a career in the Navy. The majority, however, were like me: from poor or dysfunctional families, in the Navy to avoid the draft and learn a trade or get the GI Bill to pay for a college education. Very few "rich kids" were in the ranks on the Kitty Hawk.

I was not "lifer" material, either. For me, the "Shitty Kitty" was a prison, right down to the gray steel walls, overbearing supervision, claustrophobic lack of privacy, and mindless routine. I missed freedom and music and joy, and I had begun to think about cross-dressing again.

It was briefly at first, a few momentary mental lapses, fleeting daydreams which I quickly suppressed. But more and more frequently I snapped awake to discover I had been staring at a bulkhead for some unknown period of time, envisioning scenes of that other life.

Yes, I thought to myself, I live in a gray prison, but my dreams unfold in full, glorious color.

Survival, however, required that I keep the girl inside me prisoner as well. For my own safety, I had to lock her up in a cage. But gradually, despite my efforts, she made her presence known to me, like a big cat, pacing back and forth behind the iron bars, waiting for an opportunity, an unguarded moment.

One came.

As I had learned in boot camp, I used pantyhose to polish my boots to a high sheen. In a moment of weakness before I left home, I stuffed not one, but two pairs of pantyhose into my sea bag—one pair for my boots, and one pair for me.

One evening after a difficult watch, I lay in my rack in the dim compartment staring blankly at the pipes and cables over my head. I had been looking through a Playboy magazine, gazing at the perfect bodies and wishing with all my heart that I could be them.

I often played a little game with myself. I pretended that I would magically become one of the women on the next page of the magazine. If there was more than one photograph, I'd pick one and live her life, look like her, everything. I'd be her, free and complete. It only lasted a moment, that fantasy; then it was gone, gray steel bulkheads in its place.

The compartment was quiet with steady breathing and occasional snoring around me. Despite the monstrous risk of discovery, I slowly let myself out of my bunk and stepped over to the bulkhead where my duffel bag was stored. I quietly rummaged around inside until I found my shine kit. Picking up my boondockers in case anyone was watching, I climbed back into my bunk as if I were going to shine them, and closed the privacy curtain.

Pulling the clean pair of pantyhose out of my kit, I carefully rolled each leg of the hose down to the toe, then drew them on over my feet. Leaning back in my bunk, I pulled them up past my thighs to my waist. I sat up and closed my eyes, letting the silky tightness of the hose flood through me.

Oh my god, it's been so long! I thought as I lay there. Maybe I could get a bra next time we go into port?

Holy shit, fool! There's no reason you should have a bra in your gear. Suppose they pull a surprise inspection looking for drugs? Do you have any idea what would happen to you? Do you?

I lay in my bunk behind the thin privacy curtain, terrified but unwilling to give up those few minutes of bliss, of escape, of wholeness. But I knew I dare not stay like that for long.

Reluctantly, I pulled the pantyhose off, stashing them back in the bag. I retrieved my can of shoe polish and an old t-shirt and slowly polished my boots. After all, I had to keep up appearances.

Sometime later a sailor turned up missing. His photo was posted throughout the ship, but no one knew his whereabouts. Most thought he had fallen overboard. Soon afterward, a rumor surfaced that the missing sailor had made a pass at one of his shipmates, and that in retaliation a gang of them had summarily tossed the "damn queer" overboard one dark night.

Months later, I received a letter from my sister Brenda. I had never before received a letter from one of my sisters.

Dear Rich:

I hope you're doing okay and having fun in the Navy. It's not much fun here, because there's been some changes.

I don't know if Mom has told you yet, but she and Elmer are getting a divorce. Elmer got drunk again, but this time he was real mad about something, and he hit her. She called the police. He moved out the next day.

Grampa was his usual self about it. He actually said "I told you so," to Mom's face while I was there. They got into an argument, and now Grampa has kicked us out of the house too. Mom is out looking for an apartment.

On top of all that, Barbara has run away again and we don't know where she is. We hope she comes back, but I think Mom said that if they catch her, this time they'll put her in a hospital for a while.

I'm sorry to send you bad news, but I thought you should know what's going on.

Brenda

I was released from active duty on December 12th, 1968. I returned to Kansas City, but it was a changed world from the one I had left.

Mom had found an apartment and moved on with her life, along with Brenda. Barbara was in a state hospital. Elmer was gone, searching for another unfortunate woman to marry him. And Grampa? He remained alone in his dark bunker, reading his special newspaper, waiting for the Commie apocalypse to come knocking on his door.

Thirteen

The Farmhouse - 1969

Back in "The World," as we called it, conflict over the war, civil rights unrest, the Women's Liberation movement, and all manner of protest and struggle permeated the culture, polarizing it, splitting friends and families apart. There was no middle ground; you were either for or against, a sexist pig or a drugged-out hippie. I dropped back into this cultural maelstrom as if by parachute, and hastily sought shelter in the familiar. I scurried home to Kansas City and found a job with the city reading water meters, while I enrolled in night school at the University.

Many of my high school acquaintances had deferments. Two of them, Owen and his brother Michael, along with their girlfriends, had leased a large, two-story country house on the outskirts of town while I had been busy fighting the Communist aggressors. It had nine bedrooms, multiple fireplaces, a large great room, and a carriage house. We called it The Farmhouse. In March of 1969 they invited me to move in and share the rent.

Located on the main floor near the entrance, my fifteen-by-fifteen-foot bedroom had a small marble fireplace on the outside wall. In its day, it might have been a parlor for meeting guests. I moved in and happily began redecorating.

I bought a metal bed frame at the second-hand store and cut a piece of heavy plywood to fit, plopping a twin mattress on top. I added a wool blanket the Navy had kindly given me and a light quilt, plus sheets from home. Standing next to the bed was another second-hand store treasure, a two-headed metal gooseneck lamp. One cone-shaped fixture curved toward the ceiling to light the room, the other pointed to my bed so I could read at night.

Like many returning sailors, I'd purchased a fancy reel-to-reel stereo system while in Japan. This I positioned on wooden crates across the room.

To give the room a homey feel, I covered the ancient bowed plaster walls with wide swaths of coarse tan burlap. The rough texture and earthy smell that filled the room were so different from gray steel bulkheads; it felt welcoming.

The urge to let the girl out who had been caged for so long was back in full force now. It was not lost on me that one of the live-in girlfriends was close to my size. Twice in those early months I sneaked upstairs to check out the girl's closets, hoping to find something that fit me.

Even as I did so, I was appalled at the depths to which I had sunk. These were my friends from high school, people I had gone to parties with, whose families were known to me.

I stopped. It was too low, too disgusting. I looked at myself in the mirror and thought of a new word to add to my sick, perverted resume'.

Depraved.

❦

I held a can of cheap beer against my stomach as I slouched in front of the fireplace in the large dining room. A raucous party with at least fifty people churned around me. Iron Butterfly howled at us through big speakers, heavy with bass and drums, telling us we were "Ina Gadda Da Vida, Baby." Rumor was that the words were supposed to be "In the Garden of Eden," but the songwriter was so wasted he slurred the words when it was first recorded. It stuck.

Centered on the mantelpiece in front of me were old, painted words in a flowery script: *"A world of strife shut out, a world of love shut in."* It might have been written a hundred years ago, for all we knew. The words had been there when Owen and Michael moved in. It seemed so incongruous a sentiment amidst the howling of the speakers and the smells of old beer and fresh pot mingling in the air.

As I sat, a quiet island in a throbbing sea, I wondered what the world must have been like when those words were painted. Simpler, certainly, but perhaps naive. Or maybe wiser than us. Strife goes wherever it damn well pleases. As for love, well, we're Ina Gadda Da Vida, Baby, ain't we?

"You were in Vietnam?" the guy next to me suddenly blurted, acid in his tone.

I turned to look at him through a beery haze. I didn't know him. He was yet another fuzzy-faced, long-haired flower child, oblivious and trendy in his dirty bell-bottoms jeans and tie-dyed tee-shirt. There was even a leather vest. He smelled of weed.

"Yeah," I replied. "I was on a carrier in the Gulf of Tonkin. I did the weather."

"Shit, man," he said, slurring his words, leaning in. "Then you were just a tool of the military-industrial complex. You prob'ly did just as much to kill innocent people over there as any grunt. Just another kind of baby-eater. Why'd you go?"

I stared at him for a moment, wondering if he was for real. Wondering, through the beer, if he had actually just called me a "baby eater" to my face. Really, I thought, you rich little fuck? Did daddy get you out of the draft with his money?

"I needed the GI Bill to go to school," I replied. "So how come you didn't get drafted?" I asked, testing my theory.

"Oh, I'm a student at the University so I got a deferment. I'm majoring in political science, and I've learned all about how capitalism works, preying on the workers to make just a few corporate dogs rich."

He started to go on, but I interrupted.

"Say, I'm curious. What does your father do?"

"Umm, he's a lawyer," was the somewhat puzzled reply. "Anyway, it is the capitalists who run this country, ya know. The war is a trumped-up...."

There is such a huge gulf between us, I thought, as he burbled on and on. He, the son of privilege, is sitting here passing judgment on the rest of us great unwashed. I'd like to rip that silver spoon right out of his mouth and shove it up his ass.

Instead, I turned back to my beer and the mantelpiece. Why am I so angry? I know the war is wrong. But I had to do the job, do what was expected of me. I needed to get away from home, I needed the GI Bill. I didn't have options, unlike this fool. None.

Rich assholes. Fuck 'em all.

But instead of fighting back, instead of laying into him like a "real man" would have, tears suddenly came to my eyes. I wiped them away just as someone walking by glanced at me. He stopped.

"Why are you crying?"

The political scientist quickly responded for me. "He was in Vietnam, and now he realizes what he's done."

A few months later Ina Gadda was gone, replaced by Creedence Clearwater Revival pouring out of the speakers. Bad Moon Rising, they said. Yup, I thought, drunk again, bad moon. A moment later the bad moon reached my throat and I hustled out the front door to throw up.

Deciding that I had had enough to drink for the night, I stumbled back to my room, weaving my way down the hall. I stepped into my dark bedroom without turning on the light, closing the door behind me. As I fumbled with my belt buckle, a soft noise intruded my blurry consciousness.

There's someone in my bed!

Trying to stay upright and tread quietly, I moved over to the bed. It was a girl. I didn't know her.

"Well, hi Goldilocks," I muttered. It was too noisy and public to go back out into the house, so I decided to crash as best I could. After all, it wasn't like I was going to have any difficulty getting to sleep, and it was my room, after all. I went back out to the hallway and pulled a winter jacket from the hall closet. Creeping back into the room, I lay down on a small throw rug next to the bed, draping the jacket over my shoulders. I rested my head on my arm and fell asleep almost immediately.

Sometime later, a hand shook me. I looked up. The girl was leaning over the edge of the bed. In the darkness I could make out blonde hair in a page boy style.

"This your room?" she asked.

"Yeah."

"Sorry, I needed a place to crash," she offered. "I hope that's okay."

"Thass all right," I slurred back.

After a short pause, she said, "Okay, take off your shoes and get up here," indicating the space beside her. I hesitated, then pulled off my shoes and got up off the floor.

"I'm Richard," I said by way of introduction.

"I'm Barb," she replied. I climbed into the bed, put my back to her, and fell instantly back to sleep.

Morning came early, and the night before pounded its message of excess into my head. My stomach, at least, was empty, but my bladder was not.

I still lay in the same position, my back to the girl in my bed. Barb, isn't it? I carefully moved off the bed to the floor. She was still sleeping.

I padded to the bathroom near the kitchen, washed up quickly, and went back to my room where I found her sitting on the edge of the bed.

"Umm, hi there," I said as I entered. "It's Barb, right?"

"Yes, that's right, I'm Barbara Logan." She extended her hand. "You're Richard, as I remember."

"Yes, I'm Richard Shepard," I responded, reaching out to shake her hand in return.

Her warm hand and long, graceful fingers fit my hand perfectly. Even sitting, she was tall and thin-boned. She wore glasses, giving her a bookish look. Behind the glasses, her brownish-hazel eyes had a gentle softness to them. Friendly eyes.

Hoping to relieve the somewhat awkward situation, I quipped, "Come here often?" as our hands dropped.

She smiled at my stupid joke. She appreciated the effort.

"No, not very," she replied. "My friend and I heard about the party, so we decided to come and see what it was all about. My friend ended up spending the night with one of your roommates, Owen was his name I think, so I needed to crash somewhere. We came in her car."

"No problem," I said. "So, why don't we head out to the kitchen, make some coffee and see what's to eat. I'll show you where the bathroom is on the way."

While she freshened up, I set up a pot of coffee and rummaged through my food stash in one of the two communal refrigerators. I had eggs and a package of bacon. That'll be enough, I thought, and put a skillet on the stove top to start the bacon. I had just turned over the first batch when she emerged.

"Feeling better?" I asked.

She nodded as she sat down at the table. "Yes, much better."

"I've got bacon and eggs and coffee, if that's all right," I said.

"That's just perfect," she responded, and walked over to the coffee pot to pour herself a cup. "Do you have cream and sugar?" she asked.

"On the table," I said. "Have a seat. The bacon is about done, so how do you like your eggs?"

"Oh, just scrambled is fine."

A few minutes later we sat down to breakfast. We took our first sips of coffee and our first bites of food in silence. We were both hungry and thirsty, so it didn't feel awkward.

"So, what do you do?" she asked after a minute.

"I work for the Water Department as a meter reader right now," I responded, "but I'm attending night school at the University." Cautiously, not sure what kind of response I would get, I added, "I was just released from active duty with the Navy. I served on an aircraft carrier off the coast of Vietnam." I paused to see her response.

She smiled. "My dad is a retired Army Captain. Now he's a cop with the Kansas City police."

She went on. "I work as a nurse's assistant at the hospital, but I'd like to go back to school for pre-med someday, or maybe to study law to become a lawyer."

We talked, and had relaxed enough to get to know each other when her friend wandered into the kitchen. Barb introduced her, and we spoke for a bit, but it was clear she wanted to go home.

Finishing her breakfast, Barb rose from the table, saying, "I left my purse in your room. Can I get it?"

"Of course," I said, popping up from my chair. "Let's go."

As we walked, I thought furiously. I liked her. She was pretty in a nice way, obviously intelligent, and easy to talk to.

Okay, it's now or never.

"Umm, we're having another party next Friday. I think it will be much quieter than this one was. Would you like to come back?"

86

"Yes, I'd like that," she said without pausing. "Let's trade phone numbers, in case one of us has to cancel. Okay?"

"Okay," I said. It gave her a chance to back out if she had second thoughts. That was all right. I understood.

We traded numbers, then walked to the front door.

"Thank you for breakfast, Richard," she said. Then she leaned toward me quickly, giving me a kiss on the cheek. Startled, I made no move to kiss her back, and like a quick, cool breeze, she and her friend whooshed out the door.

I stood staring after her. Oh my god, she likes me!

TRANS-FORMATIONS

Fourteen

Barbara Jean - 1969

Barbara Logan occupied my thoughts constantly during the week following the party. She actually liked me, I kept reminding myself, as if by saying it again and again the demon of self-doubt would be slain.

I worried, too, about my little problem. I'd dressed just two times since moving to the Farmhouse. But no more, I told myself. If we had sex I wouldn't need to do it anymore. No worries.

Does she like me enough to want sex? I can do it, I want to do it, but only if she wants to. Should I go out and buy some condoms?

Oh my god, I don't know what to do!

Okay, yeah, I'll get some condoms, and more breakfast groceries, just in case. Better get the lubricated kind. I'll wash the sheets on my bed, too. And I'll slow down on the beer when she comes. I'll be good.

What should I wear? I should get some snacks. Does she like wine? I didn't see her drink, so I don't know if she drinks beer or wine. I'll get both. White or red? Okay, I'll get both, I'll be ready for anything. I'll be ready.

89

Oh hell—what if she doesn't come?

ॐ

"Hi, Barb," I said as she walked in the door, my heart skipping little beats.

It was Friday night, one week after we first met in bed. For hours it seemed I had been peeking out the front door, hoping to see her car roll down the long driveway. And now, here she was. She came with her friend again. Apparently she and Owen had had a good time last week too.

Barbara smiled at me. "Hi Richard, nice to see you again. How's the party going this time?"

"Much quieter than last week," I replied, smiling back. "Just four or five other couples here tonight. When it's like this we mostly sit around and talk. We've got some food, wine and beer if you like."

"That sounds good, I'm hungry."

We went into the kitchen, where snacks and drinks were laid out on the table. We filled paper plates with chips and hot dogs, and while she poured herself a glass of white wine, I retrieved a beer from the refrigerator.

We moved outside where half a dozen chairs of various vintages were scattered around an old wooden wire reel from the phone company that functioned as the Farmhouse picnic table. We settled down next to each other in the late afternoon sun, sipping our drinks and talking.

"I'm glad you came again," I said, starting the conversation a bit awkwardly.

"Yeah," she smiled. "Not many people sleep together first, then introduce themselves the next morning."

Her smile was genuine, spreading over her whole face, while revealing small, white teeth that leaned inward a bit. She seemed self-conscious of them, and put her hand in front of her mouth as she laughed.

"Yeah, just a bit unusual," I agreed. "So, you said you work as a nurse's aide?"

She went on to explain that she was working in a local hospital, but lived at home to save money. As an "Army Brat" she was born at Fort Lewis in Washington State, but her family moved a lot over the years. She had lived in Hawaii, Chicago, and even Germany for a while until her father retired in Kansas City. She had two sisters, one older and one younger.

"How about your family?" she eventually asked.

"Okay, umm, my family is a bit of a mess," I replied. I went on to describe our lives and its twists and turns.

She pressed her lips together when I told her about our Dad, but the eyes behind the glasses showed concern and sympathy. She has nice eyes, I noticed. Yes, hazel eyes, but browner than mine. And what marvelously high cheekbones!

"It doesn't sound like you had much of a childhood," she said. "My Dad is kinda mean, too, like you'd expect from a cop or old military policeman. He was wounded in Korea, and came back, well, changed. Angry."

We paused for a quiet moment, eating our food and sipping our drinks, contemplating our fathers while absorbing the sunset glow through the trees that surrounded the Farmhouse.

"How did you end up living out here?" she asked. "This is quite the place."

"Yeah, it sure is," I replied. "Rumor has it that it was an inn on the Santa Fe Trail, but it's built more like some rich person's mansion with all the bedrooms, extra kitchen, and carriage house. It's now owned by a big real estate developer in town. I think they're gonna tear it down someday, which will be sad. Meanwhile, my friends Owen and Mike leased it, and we all split the rent and utilities. I moved in right after I got back from active duty."

"Active duty," she responded. "So, why did you pick the Navy?"

"Actually, I have to say my Mom picked it," I replied with a wry grin.

I told her about Elmer, and the special program through the Naval Air Reserve that allowed me to finish high school.

"What was your job in the Navy?" she asked.

"I was a meteorological observer – a 'weather guesser' - on the Kitty Hawk, an aircraft carrier. We operated in the Gulf of Tonkin off the coast of Vietnam. I handled the weather reports from the pilots over the target areas."

"Wow," she said. "So you escaped your family the hard way. My older sister escaped too. She got married, and Daddy doesn't like her husband much. There were some terrible arguments."

"Funny how that is," I responded, shaking my head.

"Yes, that's sure the truth," she said. "Anyway, have you chosen a major in school yet? You said you were starting night school this fall."

"Well, I'm thinking about geology. As a kid I liked science and collecting rocks and being outside, so maybe there's a career of some kind in it. But night school is just the required courses like English and History and such. Once I get them out of the way I'll have to go to school full time to get my degree. Thankfully I've got the GI Bill to help."

"And how about your plans?" I asked. "Are you going back to school?"

"Not for a while," she responded. "I'm trying to save money, too. For now, I like working at the hospital, but it doesn't pay much. I've been looking around for something better."

In the house, someone put on some music, and a few couples were dancing. I looked at Barbara for a moment, then hesitantly asked, "Would you like to dance?"

"Umm, no thanks," she said, looking at me. "It's just that, um, I hate to dance."

I laughed out loud, relieved. "I hate it too! It makes me feel so self-conscious, like everyone is watching me being an idiot to music!"

We paused for a moment, happily listening to the rock and roll blaring inside as we relished not dancing to it. We simply sat, relaxed in each other's company.

A few minutes later she turned to me.

"It's getting a little cool out here now that the sun is almost down. Could you get me a jacket or something?"

"Sure," I said, "I'll be right back." I popped out of my chair and went back into the house to get a coat for her, wondering what might be next. I liked her, I realized. She's nice looking and smart and open and we're kinda on the same path right now. I don't even feel self-conscious around her, like I can just be myself and it'll be all right. I don't have to play the game so much.

When I returned with a jacket for her and sweater for myself, our chairs had been moved closer together.

I draped the jacket over her shoulders, then sat down next to her.

"Thanks," she said.

We sat for a long moment, without speaking, watching the light from the sun fade. A few fireflies braved the early evening, drifting in the cooling air. Turning to me, Barbara gently put her hand on my wrist. Her touch sent a sudden, stirring chill right through me.

"This is nice," she said, looking at me. "Thank you for inviting me."

"I'm glad you came," I said. "To be honest, I've wondered all week if you'd come back."

"And I wondered if you wanted me to come back," she replied. "Isn't it funny how we churn such things up in our minds? It can make you crazy."

We both laughed, each of us feeling our connection building as we continued to talk.

I'd already said things to her that I wouldn't say to another girl, yet there we were, talking without judging, showing our feelings without worrying that the other might take offense.

Gradually, the light of day faded, leaving only gray shadows in the twilight and cool air of the soft May evening. We sipped our drinks, speaking of many things: our parents and siblings, our hopes and plans, politics and religion, the price of pizza and the colors of the stars. We learned about each other, sharing the small and large parts of our lives that made us who we were. Evening became night, but we continued to talk in that soft and special darkness.

In a moment of silence, I cautiously placed my hand on her arm, leaning toward her. "May I kiss you?" I whispered, terrified.

She said nothing, but reached up to my face and led me to her lips. They were cool with the night, soft and caring, tasting of white wine. Behind us the music had changed. Someone had put on the new album by the Beatles, a slow, loving song. "Something in the way she moves," sang Paul McCartney, in a high, reedy voice.

Oh, yes.

In the darkness she put her hand in mine, saying softly, "Let's refill our drinks and go to your room. Would that be okay?"

My heart jumped.

After a pause to collect myself, I replied. "Yes, that would be very okay."

TRANS-FORMATIONS

Fifteen

Visitors - 1970

"Thank you, sir, we'll take it," I said. We stood outside a small two-bedroom bungalow in an older part of town and shook hands with our new landlord.

Barb and I had been living together for almost a year, and I had nearly lost the urge to cross-dress.

We had decided to move away from the Farmhouse, with its wild parties and communal living. She had gotten a good job in downtown Kansas City as regional manager for a non-profit organization. I still worked for the water department as a meter reader. We were happy and doing well, although our parents weren't too pleased that we were living together without being married. We didn't care. It was 1970 after all, not the dark ages of the 50s.

As our new landlord drove away, we hugged each other. "Okay, let's go shopping!" Barb exclaimed. "We need a new bed, a television, dishes, everything! Let's go to Goodwill and see what they've got. This will be fun!"

"Yes," I replied. "Let's go to that new McDonald's for a burger to celebrate!"

"That was a great breakfast," Barb said, leaning back in her chair. "Thanks."

"No problem," I replied. "Just bacon and eggs and spuds for a lazy Sunday morning."

As she smiled, there was a knock at the door.

"What?" I said, puzzled. "On Sunday morning?"

I padded over to the front door and leaned down to look through the spyhole. "It's my Mom! Oh my gosh, I hope everything's all right!" I quickly unlocked the door, pulling it open with a rush.

"Mom, are you okay?"

"Everything's fine, Richard," she replied, a smile on her face. "I was just in the neighborhood, and thought I'd drop by to see how you and Barbara were doing."

"Umm, okay," I said, a bit puzzled. "Glad to hear it. Uh, why don't you come in for a cup of coffee? We just finished breakfast, but would you like anything?"

I didn't know what to say. Most mothers didn't show up at their son's doorstep on a Sunday morning—especially when the son lives with his girlfriend.

"Yes, a cup of coffee would be nice," she said as she stepped into the house. "Ah, hello Barbara. How are you?"

"I'm just fine, Margaret, how are you? Is everything okay?"

"Everything's fine. I was just in the neighborhood."

"That's great," Barb replied, also a bit puzzled. "I'm glad you dropped by. I'll go put on a new pot."

For the next twenty minutes we sat in the living room, awkwardly talking about nothing. The weather was fine, the daffodils were blooming, her work was fine, everything was fine.

"Well, thank you for the coffee. I should be going." Mom stood up, picking up her purse and moving toward the door. Hugging first Barb then me, she said, with a smile on her face, "You take care of yourselves now. Come by my place for a visit sometime."

"Sure Mom, we will. Thanks for dropping by." And with that, she was out the door.

After the door closed, Barb and I looked at each other.

"What was that all about?" I said.

"I think she was checking us out—checking me out," Barb replied. "She was doing her Mom thing."

"I guess you're right, but I'm glad that's over."

An hour later while I was at the kitchen sink washing the breakfast dishes, there was a knock at the door.

Barb came out of the bathroom where she had just finished her shower. She had her clothes on, but her hair was still wet. With a dish towel in my hands, I went to the front door.

It was Barb's parents, Wyatt and Mildred, standing on the front stoop.

"Hey there, Rick, how the hell are ya!" Wyatt bellowed. He was a bit deaf from his time in the Army, so he always spoke loudly.

"Hi Wyatt, hi Mildred, I'm fine. Come on in. What brings you out this way?"

"Aww, we were just in the neighborhood and thought we'd check on ya," he said, a smile on his face. "Got any coffee?"

For the next twenty minutes we sat in the living room, awkwardly talking about nothing. Then, abruptly, as if on a secret signal, Wyatt and Mildred stood up and moved toward the door.

"Well, kids, we gotta go. You guys be good!" Wyatt yelled as they bustled out the door.

The quiet that filled the house as the front door closed still vibrated with Wyatt's voice. Barb and I just looked at each other, exhausted by their visit.

"Let's just sit in front of the tube for a while." I suggested.

"Sounds good to me."

We were deep into a repeat of Wild Kingdom—Musk-ox in Alaska—when we heard a knock at the door.

"I'll get it," Barb said.

"Why, hello Mr. Fristoe. What brings you to this neighborhood?" She turned her head to call back to me. "It's your grandfather, Rich."

"Well, hi Grampa. What a surprise. Come in, can we get you anything?"

His taciturn voice responded, "I wouldn't mind a cup of tea. I was just in the neighborhood, and thought I'd see how you were faring. I hope I'm not intruding."

Yes, he said, the farm was fine, the crops had been planted without difficulty, just hope we didn't get too much rain or a flood. There were no problems, the levee was in good shape, we could go down there this summer if we wanted, everything was fine, just fine. Had I noticed that the daffodils were blooming?

"Oh. My. Gawd," I said, as we stood on the front sidewalk watching Grampa drive away.

100

"That's for sure," Barb responded. "You know they were in this together, don't you? They don't like it that we're living together. This was their way of telling us without actually saying it."

"Yeah, that's pretty clear. They've sure made their opinions known, haven't they?"

I looked at Barb, contemplating the question that our parents had just unceremoniously dumped in our laps.

It's not just about sex; we connect at many levels, I realized. I hadn't had a strong urge to cross-dress since I met her. It appeared my little problem was solved after all.

Yes, I decided, it's gone, and I can't imagine anything better than spending my life with this woman.

I turned to face her. Taking her hands in mine, standing in the front yard of our shabby little rental house on a sunny Sunday, May 3rd, 1970, I said:

"Barbara, will you marry me?"

She paused a moment, then smiled. "Yes, Richard, I will."

"Wonderful!" I said, grinning like an idiot.

We arranged to be married at the county courthouse on Friday.

Monday night we called our friends. Tuesday night I gave Mom the news in person. I couldn't tell if she was happy or sad. She just said "I'll be there," and left it at that.

Wednesday night, when we had told Barb's parents we were getting married, Wyatt made it clear he was happy his middle daughter was marrying another veteran, not one of those damn draft dodgers or hippies. He's only a "swabbie," he said when he thought I didn't hear him, "but that's enough."

❧

"It's a shotgun wedding!" Wyatt boasted in a loud voice, pulling his sport jacket away to show off his badge and service revolver.

We nervously stood in the small outer office of one Judge Mazuch. In attendance were Wyatt and Mildred, my Mom, Grampa, Barb's two sisters, and four of our friends from high school. Judge Mazuch was an acquaintance of Wyatt's who agreed to perform the ceremony. Apparently, he did a lot of them.

At the appointed time, a wizened little man in judge's robes emerged from the side door.

"Are you ready?" he asked in a raspy voice, looking at Barb and me.

"Yessir," I replied, nodding.

"Yessir," Barb replied, nodding.

"Okay. Dearly beloved, we are gathered here...." he began even as he moved to stand behind the desk in the middle of the little office. His words poured forth with such speed they were almost unintelligible. Barb and I managed to recognize our respective "Do You Take This Man/Do You Take This Woman" questions, notable only by a rise in inflection and brief pause in the torrent of words.

In two minutes, it was done.

We were married. It was Friday, May 8th, 1970, my 22nd birthday. Barb was 21. A minute or two later, as we were being congratulated, the judge tugged at my sleeve.

"That'll be twenty dollars, and you need to get out of here. I've got another wedding to perform."

Things changed little over the next two years. Barb continued in her job recruiting at-risk kids for Job Corps as I went to night school and continued at the water department. I even got a promotion from meter reader to the collections division. My new job was to turn off the water to houses with unpaid bills.

It paid better, but there were some risks.

"You get the fuck off my property!" the man yelled angrily, waving a shotgun in my direction. Without a word, I turned back to my vehicle, stowed my tools in the trunk, and pulled away, shaking. I drove on to my next stop, marking the last one as "risky" in the notes. I'd come back with a cop next time.

"Hi sweetie, how was your day?" I greeted Barb from the kitchen as she got home after work.

"I had a good one, Rich, how 'bout you?"

"Not great. I had another customer show off his gun when he figured out why I was there," I said, shaking my head.

"Rich, you gotta get out of that job. I know it pays more, but somebody might hurt you one of these days," she said, a worried look on her face.

"Yeah, I've been thinking a lot about that." I paused for a moment, stirring the pot of chili I had made for dinner. "What would you say to me going back to school full time? I'm thinking I'd like to get that degree in geology."

"I think that'd be great. You've always loved rocks and being outside. You'd be good at it."

We discussed the possibility over dinner, knowing that the burden of supporting us while I was a student would fall on Barb. At least I had the GI Bill to help. Further down the road it also meant that I'd be away from home a lot, but Barb encouraged me.

Like me, she was looking to a future career. We agreed. It was the right thing to do for both our futures.

"I love you," I said softly over an empty bowl of chili. "I really, really, really do."

She smiled. "I love you too."

"I promise to do the same for you," I emphasized. "When we're settled, you can go back to college or do anything you want. Fair is fair. We're equals. Okay?"

"Agreed."

Three months later I became a full-time student at the University of Missouri—Kansas City. We rented a cheap house within walking distance of the campus, where I started classes full-time in the fall of 1973.

Sixteen

Alaina - 1974

I looked up when Barb's car pulled in the driveway, pushing back from the massive oak desk we had picked up at the second-hand store. I stood, stretching, stiff and a little bleary-eyed from studying for a chemistry exam. The smell of beef stew simmering on the stove filled the air.

"Hi sweetie," I called as she opened the back door into the kitchen.

"How'd it go today?"

"It was a good one today," she replied, hanging her purse and coat on a hook in the little entryway. "I signed up a new girl for Job Corps. She'll start in a month."

"Hey, well done!" I exclaimed. "That's what, three for the month so far, isn't it? And you've got another ten days to go."

"Yeah, it's been a good month," she grinned. "Anyway, whatcha cookin'?"

"Beef stew this time," I said. "I picked up some dinner rolls to go with it. We can eat any time you want."

A half hour later we were on the old couch in front of the television with our food and glasses of wine on TV trays.

"And that's the way it is," Walter Cronkite intoned as we ate, "Today, March 19th, 1974."

The news had been full of the Watergate scandal and the pressure on President Nixon to resign, economic fallout from the Arab oil embargo last year, and a slew of continuing crises in the Middle East. The ringing of the phone was a surprising interruption.

"I'll get it," Barb said, getting up from the couch.

"Hello? Oh hi, Alaina. Is everything all right? Slow down, slow down! Now, tell me what happened!"

Alaina, one of our neighbors, was a refugee from Czechoslovakia. She had managed to escape the Soviet invasion back in 1968, and had moved to the United States. Married to Pieter, a tall, handsome Swede, she was beautiful herself, a dark-haired Slav with hazel eyes. They seemed the perfect European couple.

"He said that?" Barb said into the phone. I could hear Alaina in the background, sobbing.

"Okay," Barb said into the phone, looking at me. "You throw together some things and get over here. You can stay in our spare bedroom. We'll deal with the rest of it later. You want one of us to come get you? Are you sure? Okay, but if we don't see you in the next thirty minutes, we're coming over. Got it? Thirty minutes. Yes, see you soon. Goodbye."

Barb hung up the phone, then plopped down on the sofa.

"Well, dammit," she spat. "Pieter has been stepping out on her. She just found out, and they had a terrible argument. She's got nowhere to go."

"Of course," I said, "She can stay here as long as she wants. I'll get the room ready, or do you want me to go get her?"

"I'll get her. I think she'd be more comfortable talking to a woman right now, okay?"

"I understand," I replied.

Alaina arrived safely that evening, and over the next few days we helped gather her things and brought them over to the house. We gave her the spare bedroom, moving my big oak desk out to the dining room.

As I was moving boxes and Alaina was putting away clothes, she opened a box and pulled out a wig. Sitting on a Styrofoam head stand, it glowed, almost metallic, with shoulder-length straight hair in a silvery blonde hue.

I stood motionless, too stunned to move. The urge to see what I would look like wearing it, to try it on, assaulted me. The girl in me, long suppressed, was screaming, desperate to see the light of day, to have just one moment of freedom—an hour, a half-hour, anything.

"Please, oh please," she pleaded.

For an endless week, I fought it. No! I shouted to myself over and over, no, no, no! You stopped that long ago. You're married now, you're doing fine. Your sex life is fine, you're going to school, you're gonna have a career. Don't risk all that, don't risk your entire future for this. You love your wife, dammit. Don't go there. Just don't!

"Oh, you've got to try it," she whispered back. "Just for a moment, just this once. No one will find out, and you want to know, don't you? It will be your only chance, ever. Just a few minutes, that's all. Just let me out for a few tiny minutes."

One morning, the opportunity came, as I knew it would. Barb was at work, Alaina meeting with her lawyer. I had two hours, perhaps a bit more. Enough. More than enough.

I moved to the closet, my mind racing, palms sweaty.

Carefully I scanned through Barb's clothes, hanger after hanger. I picked out a dress that looked like it might fit me—a polyester knit summer sheath dress, white with small colorful flowers strewn in an angled swath from shoulder to hem. It smelled of her perfume, Shalimar. I left a space where it had hung in the closet, and noted the direction it had been hanging, then turned and laid it on the bed.

Next, I moved to her dresser drawer, the top one. She had one bra that was old, stretched out and shapeless enough that I thought it might fit me. I won't use her panties, I resolved, that would be too much. Bending down, from the bottom drawer I pulled out a pair of my own briefs and white cotton socks to fill the bra cups, plus a pair of old panty hose.

I turned to the closet again, scanning Barb's shoe collection. She had a pair of light blue leather sandals with small sequin flowers. I might be able to get my feet in those if I loosen the straps, I thought.

I sat down on the bed and began with the panty hose, rolling them up my leg. I then connected the bra around my belly, turning it around to slip on the shoulder straps. I wadded up the socks, stuffing them inside, molding them to look like breasts.

I stood, turned, and then leaned down to pick up the dress, feeling the weight of the bra and socks. It felt like the bra was holding warm breasts against my chest.

I can feel her now. Her freedom is close, so close. Each item I put on is a turn of the key, unlocking the rusty iron cage door. I am not putting on women's clothes, I am freeing the woman inside.

I felt like crying, like screaming. It was the screech of painted fingernails on a chalkboard crying out no and yes at the same time, over and over.

I paused, then took a deep breath. Being careful not to damage the dress, I pulled it over the top of my head, wriggling my shoulders to get it down around my waist, pulling the hem down to a point just above my knees.

The feeling was overwhelming—the cool, smooth touch of the fabric, the feel of being encased with softness, the faint fragrance of Barb's perfume. It was as if I had been holding my breath for years, and suddenly found myself on a cool, green hilltop overlooking the sea, the breeze softly caressing my face.

I stood still, head back, eyes closed, breathing. I felt the hose and the bra, the sad breasts and the happy dress, all of it.

Just breathing.

After a minute, I moved into the bathroom. Barb's makeup was strewn across the counter. Memorizing each item's exact location, I began.

Foundation. Okay, that's first. Use the little sponge. Then a little powder, not too much, blend it in. Mascara next, with perhaps a little dark shadow on the upper eyelid. Then lipstick. Just like Barb, just like Mom. Lipstick is last.

Back to the bedroom. I sat down to put on the sandals, counting the holes in the straps so I could buckle them back to their original position. The toe was a bit narrow, but I could just close the buckle. Standing up, I looked down, past the lumpy breasts, beyond the hem of the dress, to my feet, barely contained by the lovely, sparkling blue sandals.

Oh god. Time for the wig.

I walked into the spare bedroom, now Alaina's room, walking clumsily in the tight shoes. The wig sat on a bookcase, gleaming. I reached over and picked it up. To my surprise, the Styrofoam head came with it. It was pinned to the head. Carefully memorizing where the pin was inserted, I removed it, then lifted the wig and returned to our bedroom. The dresser mirror was the largest mirror in the house, and I wanted to see myself.

Complete and whole, I needed to see myself.

Bending my head down, I pulled the wig over my head, making it snug, then lifted up my head to look in the mirror. The wig was too far down on my forehead and twisted off to one side. I looked ridiculous. I leaned close to the mirror, adjusting it until it looked about right, then stepped back.

A young woman looked back at me from the mirror. A little broad in the shoulders, small breasts, but lean. The lively, clingy dress created curves where none existed before. The silky hair arched over the jaw line, and the bangs drifted down the forehead to feather the eyebrows. Hazel eyes, sad eyes, yes, but now sparkling, brilliantly alive. The makeup just right, not too much, giving the illusion of elegance, of control.

I stared at her, at myself. Could anyone love that person, that woman? Could I be loved? Or am I just a twisted pervert, looking ridiculous to anyone who would see me. They wouldn't see a girl or a woman; they'd see some kind of warped and wretched creature.

But maybe not. Maybe I could find love with a man? No, I'm not attracted to men. A woman? That would make me a lesbian, but that's okay. Yes, a woman, one who would see the real me, care for the real me, never laugh at me or demean me. We'd cuddle, comfortably watching a movie, sipping a little wine as the evening drifted into night. She'd kiss me on the cheek now and again, just because. Then, when the movie was over, we'd turn off the television, dim the lights, and slowly, gently, make love. We'd ....

A spasm, hot and fast, spread through me. I had come. Ejaculated without an erection, my penis tucked back between my legs and into my underwear as far as I had been able to push it.

I had come.

In a flash the moment was lost. The girl in the mirror was gone, replaced by an awkward creature clacking to the bathroom to clean itself up.

Over the next half-hour, I put everything back in its place: makeup, bra, dress, wig. Then, in a daze, I went to the kitchen to start dinner.

Okay, pervert, I raged to myself, what are you going to cook up to cover your tracks? What are you going to do to atone for your lack of truthfulness to the woman you love? The girl in you is back, you know. You can't keep denying her forever. It worked for a while, but not anymore. So now, what? Put a bullet in your head? Take pills, jump off a bridge? Eventually you've got to do something.

You know that, don't you, fool? Don't you?

TRANS-FORMATIONS

Seventeen

The Oregon Trail - 1976

I graduated from UMKC with a degree in geology in 1976, and was accepted into the graduate program at Oregon State University in Corvallis. Barb and I both wanted to move away from the sultry Midwestern summers and bitterly cold winters to the cool green hills of the Pacific Northwest.

The timing was good, as Barb had reached a turning point in her career and was looking for a change. She quickly found work in Oregon with the local county as their affirmative action officer.

For me, there was one more challenge to face before full acceptance into the graduate program—the first year exam.

The first year exam was a demonic creation. The all-day written test required essay responses, not multiple choice. The questions could cover any topic in geology. All of it. I had to pass the test to stay in graduate school.

At the end of fall semester, just before Christmas break, we received a large bibliography of professional papers and references to study. "These may or may not be on the test," our professors said. Most of us new grad students, twenty-seven in all, took the hint and spent our "vacation" in the library, studying our asses off.

We took the test in January.

☙

"Ah, Rick. Come in and have a seat."

"Thanks, Dr. Field."

I was in my professor's office to learn the results from the test. Palms sweaty, stomach churning, I sat down at the chair next to his big oak desk.

"Okay, Rick, I'll get right to it." Doctor Field said. "You did well. You passed all eight sections of the test and came in third overall."

I sat for a moment, mouth slightly open.

"Uhh, thank you. I must admit, I'm stunned!"

"Yes, I can see that," he smiled. "Nevertheless, you are to be commended. I have the test here. It can't leave my office, but I encourage you to look at the professors' comments and grading in the next week or so."

"Yes sir, I will. Thank you."

"Before you go, though, I have one other matter I'd like to discuss with you.

"Yes?"

"One of my former students works in the mining and exploration business. He's putting together a crew for an exploration program in southeast Alaska this summer, and he needs field geologists. It would be four months living in a helicopter-supported bush camp near Wrangell. Might you be interested?"

"Wow! Yes sir, absolutely."

"Excellent. I'll have him call you in the next week or so. Meanwhile, go home and celebrate!"

ॐ

All I knew, I explained to Barb, was that I'd be living in a bush camp in a river valley at the foot of a place called Cone Mountain, about 25 miles east of Wrangell in the southeast panhandle of Alaska. The only way in or out was by helicopter, but we'd have radio communication with the flight service.

"What's a "bush camp?" she asked.

"I think it means we'll live in tents and get mail and supplies once a week."

"Umm, sounds a bit rough."

It promised to be rough for both of us. Four months was a long time to be apart. At least the company offered to fly wives up to Ketchikan for a three-day break over the Fourth of July, all expenses paid.

"Oh, that will be fun," she said, referring to the trip. "And you'll get paid for this?"

"Yup, 350 bucks a month. My first job in geology, sweetie, and we're rich!"

TRANS-FORMATIONS

Eighteen

Flying In - 1977

I peered through the window of the Boeing 727 as we flew northward from Seattle in the crisp morning air. Far below, tree-covered islands were scattered to the horizon, appearing to float on the silvery-blue water of Puget Sound. The islands were bristly with tall dark pines; wispy fog banks hugged bays and inlets around some of the islands, while puffy cumulus clouds billowed above others in the distance.

It's beautiful, but it sure feels like I'm going into the Navy again, I thought. I'm leaving home and nervous about what's ahead. Can I do this? Can I handle the job?

Can I go months without getting dressed?

Only time will tell.

Four hours and a bag of peanuts later, we landed in Wrangell. I filed off the plane, walking across the tarmac to the small one-gate terminal. There were a few other passengers like myself, wearing jeans, hiking boots, looking like grad students emerging from months in university libraries. We introduced ourselves.

Tim was a tall, curly-haired Irishman with a ready grin. He came from the University of Minnesota in Duluth, which he called

117

"Dull Tooth." Abe was a thin black man from Ethiopia. He attended the University of Idaho in Moscow. He had a quick, genuine smile matching his quirky sense of humor. Dean hailed from Washington State University in Pullman. The biggest of all of us, he stood a bit over six feet tall with reddish-brown hair and a serious demeanor.

I was the oldest of the group at 29, and the only married man and veteran. While I had inherited my father's thick, coppery-brown hair, the pale skin of my childhood had persisted, along with unwelcome traces of teenage acne.

We retrieved our gear from baggage claim and sat down to wait. It wasn't long before a tall man wearing a leather flight jacket walked over to us and asked, "Are you guys with the exploration crew?"

"Yes." We all nodded.

"Okay. My name's Dave, and I'm with the flying service. Grab your stuff and follow me." He led us out through a side door onto the tarmac, where he told us to pile our gear on a nearby cart. "We're going to our office over there," he said, pointing. "So drag it along."

We followed, two of us pulling the cart, two pushing, as we walked toward a low building attached to a hangar about 100 yards away. We parked the cart and went inside. While we each had a cup of bitter old coffee from Styrofoam cups, the secretary behind the counter took our names and addresses. "It's for the mail," she said. Then she asked each of us for our shoe sizes.

"Huh?" we said.

"Your company ordered new boots for each of you. They're rubber boots. Around here they're called Sitka Slippers. They're the best thing to wear in southeast Alaska where it rains so much.

I'll be phoning in the order, and the store will deliver them before you take off. Twenty minutes, tops."

They arrived, new in the box, fourteen minutes later. They were brown rubber boots with tan waffled soles, shiny as a new car with price stickers still attached. We tried them on, feeling a little foolish. They fit fine.

When we were done admiring our new footwear, Dave said, "Are you ready? Okay, then let's get the aircraft loaded."

We followed him into the hangar. He walked over to a big single-engine airplane on floats parked out front. The plane stood eight feet tall, perched on big pontoons that had wheels extending from the front and inside.

"This is it," he said.

"What kind of plane is this?" I asked.

"It's a DeHavilland Beaver," he replied. "They've been used for decades in places like Alaska and northern Canada. The wheels retract into the pontoons so we can land on water or on a runway." With that he turned to the task of sorting our gear and the supplies in cardboard boxes.

"Okay," he said, looking us over. He pointed at me and said, "You go in first and sit in the back. Then we'll load some of the lighter boxes in with you, and work forward."

I climbed up on the pontoon and through the door, crouching down to move through the plane to the last seat. A round porthole window on my left gave me a limited view outside. A growing pile of boxes blocked the view out the right side as, piece by piece and person by person, we loaded the plane using every available space. Once the loading was finished, Dave walked around the outside of the plane, checking it over, and then jumped up onto the pontoon.

119

Leaning in the door, he turned and said, "Okay, guys, fasten your seatbelts and put on those headsets hanging by your seats. It'll be too noisy in here to talk, but if you need to say something just press the switch on the cord. Got it?"

He moved into his seat with practiced ease and sat down, fastening his own belt and putting on a headset. He spent a minute checking gauges and switches; then, with the flip of a switch, the engine growled to life, shaking the plane like a big, wet dog. He spoke into his radio, and moments later we began taxiing.

Before we reached the end of the runway, we braked to a stop at an open area. Dave then grasped the throttle control and gradually pushed it forward, gunning the engine. His voice crackled through the intercom. "Engine and instrument check!" he said over the noise. He held the plane in place for about ten seconds, engine roaring, scanning gauges on the instrument panel.

Then his voice came over the headsets again. "Okay. Here we go!"

Yes, here we go, I thought, suddenly reminded of Mom and long ago Christmas lights. Goodbye, civilization!

We lifted off toward the north, banking eastward as we gained altitude. The shore beneath us gave way to ocean, foam streaming along its gray-green surface, looking very cold. As we climbed, southeast Alaska unfolded before us.

Waves pounded rocky shores. Craggy boulders and steep hillsides were covered in the deep, ragged green of pines and the lighter, softer green of alder and thick brush. Rounded rock outcrops and angular cliffs poked out here and there in huge jumbles. We will be working in that, I thought to myself.

Soaring eastward, the water below us quickly changed. No longer clean, it swirled with heavy streaks of thick brown sand and clouds of fine mud. Ahead stretched a swampy, flat bay of long, ribboned sand bars, glistening mud flats, and tangled tree stumps. We raced through the sky over the delta of the great Stikine River.

The Stikine River drained the high country of northwest British Columbia. Due to its isolation, it remained one of the last wild major rivers in North America. We flew along its course perhaps five hundred feet high, speeding east over a wide, flat valley guarded by snow-crusted ridges and peaks in the middle distance north and south of us.

Fifteen minutes later, Dave throttled the engines back.

"Everybody strapped in?" he asked over the intercom. I tightened my seat belt a bit, then looked out the little porthole. All I could see was muddy, fast-moving water and dense trees overhanging the river bank.

I watched out the porthole as we approached the surface of the water and touched down in a great spray of water accompanied by a hard bounce. We had landed on the river headed upstream against the current. As the aircraft slowed, a large sandy island came into my view about fifty yards off. We angled toward it, and soon we were positioned close to the embankment.

Dave shut off the engine. Quickly, he unbuckled, took off his headset and opened his door. He turned and stepped out of the cabin with a length of rope in his hand. He looped it to a cleat on the pontoon, then jumped the short distance to the shore, pulling the plane closer and lashing the line to a tree stump.

"Hey, Dean," he yelled. "Come stand by the line. I need to get back aboard."

Dean unbuckled and scrambled out, while Dave hopped back onto the pontoon to supervise the unloading. We formed a chain, passing boxes and gear forward.

When we and all the gear were ashore, Dave untied the rope and slid back into the pilot's seat. As the plane drifted away from the island he yelled, "The helicopter will be here for you in a while. Just hang out!" Then he closed the door and restarted the Beaver's engine.

He angled the plane into the river, turning it around to point downstream. The engine roared, throwing up spray as it sped westward, lifting out of the water and climbing away. Within minutes it dwindled to a small speck far downstream, then was gone.

A few hours ago we were buying overpriced coffee at Sea-Tac airport in Seattle, I mused as we watched him go. Now, we're perched on the edge of the world.

We stood on our island gawking at snow-capped peaks, the graceful white sweeps of snowfields like rumpled blankets on their shoulders. Here and there, the hint of blue glacial ice poked out from under the snow, glinting in the sun. Streams of icy melt-water spewed from under the ice, cascading down the bare rocks to disappear into the ragged green forest below.

The Stikine burbled all around us, thick and brown, whirl-pools and secret currents lurking beneath its filmy surface. The whine of mosquitoes came faintly to our ears, promising tortures to come. The cool, damp air smelled of mud and sand, a musty smell overlain by rotting vegetation.

There we stood—four very green college students, excited and a little apprehensive, perched on an isolated island in the middle of a wild Alaskan river, wearing our shiny new Sitka Slippers.

Nineteen

Welcome, Campers - 1977

For nearly an hour the four of us talked, sitting on the bleached old logs and gritty sand of the island, leaning against our bags.

The sounds of Alaska surrounded us, the rush of silty water in the river, the faint whine of mosquitoes, and the occasional screech of a hawk. Abruptly, a different kind of whine filled the air, accompanied by a pulsing throp-throp-throp.

The helicopter was on its way.

It raced out of a valley to the south, a small egg-shaped craft painted red and white. Swooping toward us, it dropped to a hover about five feet off the ground, gently touching down in a cacophony of high-pitched turbine noise and blowing sand.

As the whine diminished and the blades slowed, the pilot unbuckled and climbed out. "Hi, fellas. "My name's Jim."

We introduced ourselves and shook hands all around. He was about my size, with sandy hair and a thick, full beard. He wore a flat, tweedy cap that bore evidence of many hours scrunched under a headset.

"Okay," he said after introductions. "I'll be taking you up to the camp. It's about ten miles south of us on the Katete River, a tributary to the Stikine. Two people at a time with all your gear. It's a ten-minute flight, so it won't be long before I'm back for the second trip. Have any of you been in a helicopter before?"

We all shook our heads no.

"Okay, no problem. So, for this trip I'll take you, Rick, and you, Abe."

Abe and I helped load our bags into the helicopter, plus an assortment of supplies that Jim stashed under the back seat and on the floor at our feet. He showed us how to work the buckle on the multi-point seat harness and use the headset. Five minutes later we took off in another blast of sand and noise.

I sat in the back, the seat constructed of simple canvas stretched over a tubular aluminum frame. At my left ear, a large bulge in the ceiling that contained the transmission delivered power from the turbine in the back to the blades above us. Despite the padding around it and the muffling of the headset, a high-pitched metallic whine cut through the air inside the little craft.

We zipped over the forest a few hundred feet below us. Through the tall pines, the Katete River squeezed into a narrow gorge between steep rock walls. Surging white water tumbled and swirled around huge boulders and fallen trees in a ragged, frothy mass. If we had to hike out, we sure couldn't come this way, I realized.

A few minutes later we emerged from the narrow canyon into a broad, flat valley. We slowed and dropped altitude, approaching the camp that would be our home for the next four months. Two orange tents and a larger central tent of white canvas clustered together on a flat island in the middle of the river. The tents were pitched on raised plywood platforms.

We landed about fifty yards from the camp amid a group of blue 55-gallon fuel barrels. The pilot let the helicopter engine drop to idle, then unbuckled and jumped out to help us unload. It seemed odd not to have the pilot sitting at the controls while the blades still spun above us, but I learned it was a common technique for offloading and refueling.

The Katete was a "braided" stream, with multiple channels of swiftly moving water that shifted each summer in response to the surge of snow-melt runoff from the surrounding mountains. Our island stood four or five feet above the present level of the river, which ran silty gray, fast and cold. A quarter-mile wide and a mile long, the island supported no living trees, just tall brush and a few bald logs and stumps washed downriver the previous season. Because the island was open and flat, a gentle breeze blew the mosquitoes away.

The river valley itself stretched nearly a mile wide. To the east of camp stood Cone Mountain, rising 5,000 feet above the valley floor, towering over the landscape. Trees covered its lower reaches, then brush gave way to barren, cream-colored granite higher up.

To the west sat a 1,000-foot high curving wall of massive gray gneiss—a layered metamorphic rock—streaked with black lichen and exposing occasional thick cream-colored dikes cutting sharply through it. Both the mountain on one side and the gneiss wall on the other were broken by widely spaced gullies gushing with sparkling waterfalls. Snow fields arched over several gullies, glistening in the bright sun.

The camp would have all the comforts, including an electrical generator that ran on diesel fuel, a full kitchen with running water and a hot shower. But much of it had yet to be built. Randy, the geologist in charge of the program, showed us what was needed, so we picked up hammers and nails and proceeded to finish building our home. Meanwhile, Tim and Dean arrived and soon began construction work as well.

At eight o'clock, we called it a day. It felt like late afternoon at that latitude, but all of us were tired to the bone. The cook had thrown together some sandwiches, as the kitchen was not yet functional enough for a hot meal. We sat at our newly built plywood table in the big white kitchen tent and ate.

Afterwards, Randy split us into teams of two for field work. Tim from Duluth and I were paired to work and bunk together for the rest of the season. I was happy with that, as Tim seemed a likeable sort.

At last, we retired to our tents, cold beer chilled by the icy Ketete in hand. Each 10x10 wall tent had two plywood bunks with thick foam pads, a set of shelves for each of us, and an electric heater.

From the entrance to our tent, Cone Mountain towered over the camp, golden in the glow of the setting sun. Water rushed in the river and a faint, crisp breeze moved around me. It was a peaceful scene, serene and stunning to behold.

Back in the world, the news carried stories of politics and wars, tragedies and triumphs. There were bills to pay and traffic to deal with and jobs to do. Barb was now on her own, dealing with whatever happened without me. I was here facing new challenges without her. We were both in new territory.

In a single day, the ordinary concerns of our daily lives had drastically changed.

126

৵

"Okay, fellas, let's go out to the helicopter and get started," Jim said.

Finishing our morning coffee, we filed out the door into the cool Alaskan air.

"All right," he began as we sat in a semi-circle around him. "This is Five-Seven Foxtrot. That's the tail number for this particular ship. It's a Hughes 500-D model, and it's the perfect machine for the type of flying we will be doing this summer. It has a lot of power, and its five blades are somewhat shorter than those on other helicopters, which means it can fit into tighter landing areas. That also makes it more responsive and maneuverable.

"The egg shape of the reinforced cabin means that in a crash the ship will roll rather than just squash flat. Hopefully. The skids and the tail boom are designed to shear off as that happens. It'd be a hell of a ride, but we might survive."

He went on to describe how we would work around the helicopter and the safety protocols we would follow to do so safely.

"As you can see, this part of Alaska doesn't have many open, flat landing areas, especially up in the mountains where we will be working. So, to get around that and get you close to where you need to go, we are going to practice 'toe-in' landings."

"Here's how it works," Jim began, using his hands to show us. "We will fly right up to the face of the mountain in an area as clear of brush and trees as possible. I will perch the front of the helicopter skids against the ground or rock outcrop, or even a log or tree stump, whatever is available. Note that the back part of the skids will still be in the air. In fact, I will essentially be flying the helicopter into the side of the mountain."

"Then, at my signal, you will slowly climb out onto the skids, facing inward and holding on to a solid part of the ship. Don't hold on to the doors, they're thin and they'll just rip off under your weight. On the skid you will then move forward until you can step down onto the ground. At that point you will move away from the helicopter laterally, staying well clear of the rotor blades, but in a path where I can still see you.

"This whole process is choreographed so that we always know what the other person is doing. It must be done slowly so that I can compensate for your shifting weight as you move. And when I pick you up on a slope, we'll do the process in reverse."

He paused, looking at our dumbstruck faces, and grinned. "And that, guys, is a toe-in landing."

"Wow," I said. The others nodded.

"Any questions?" he said.

"Okay. Now, one more important thing to remember: we are never in a hurry. Never. Move slowly and carefully, and there'll be no problems. We'll practice this afternoon. Then I think you'll be ready for the mountain."

Twenty

Cone Mountain - 1977

"We're gonna have to split up for this one, I think," I said to Tim.

We had been collecting samples on the mountain for several weeks now, and had completed much of the grid area above the tree line. Now we worked downslope toward the scraggly pines, alder, and thick brush, where steep-sided gullies—some of them still filled with semi-permanent snow fields—cut into the mountain.

Tim took the north gully while I headed down the south, sampling every one-hundred feet as we went. It was steep going for both of us, but we were getting used to it.

The rocks on the slope were loose, wet and slippery with moss and mud. I moved from one perch to another, testing each step before I put my full weight on it.

As the morning progressed and it got warmer, I noticed that the surface of the snowfield covering the gully was melting, becoming soft enough to create a decent foothold just by jamming my foot into the snow. I realized I could make my way down on

129

the snow, then dive into the brush only where I needed to get a sample.

I moved to the edge of the snowfield and began to descend, making steps as I went. At about 100-foot intervals, I cut back into the brush. By late afternoon it was time to cross over to Tim's side of the gully to a big rock we had spotted where Jim would do a toe-in to pick us up. I made my way back to the edge, cinched up my pack, and stepped out on the snowfield to traverse across to the landing site.

I'd made it less than fifty feet from "shore" when, without warning, the snow under my left foot gave way.

I threw my body toward my right side as I fell, my left leg plunging into a void. The rest of me stayed on the surface. I laid in the snow for a long moment, my left leg dangling in the hole I'd just made.

Shit. I'd better try to see how far down it goes and which direction the crevasse extends before I try to move, I thought. I cautiously raised up on my elbow.

Past my leg, a deep chasm plunged perhaps fifty feet. The narrow, irregular crevasse ranged from four-feet wide at the top, walled in dense ice, to about one-foot wide where it narrowed toward the bottom. Below that, it disappeared into total blackness. I couldn't see how far it extended to either side.

Carefully, I rolled away to the right, crawling on my belly for a few yards. I took a chance and rose up to my hands and knees and shuffled back to the trees, dragging my pack behind me. Finally at the trees, I paused to calm my nerves and to consider my situation.

Okay, I still have to get across this thing. It's not likely there's another landing site below me. The mountain just gets steeper and the brush thicker down there. And I don't want to climb back up, as that would require a couple of hours of hard work. In either case, Jim wouldn't know where to look for me. .

I decided to chance it on the snow at a different crossing spot. But this time, I resolved, I'd be prepared.

I searched around in the trees nearby, finding a fallen tree limb about the diameter of my arm and about five feet long.

Using the shaft of my rock hammer like a blunt hatchet, I broke away the smaller branches as best I could. With the branches stripped, I slipped on my backpack, loosening the shoulder straps. I then threaded the tree limb under the straps and across my chest. I reasoned that if I fell through the snow again, the tree branch might keep me from dropping too far.

I ventured back out on the snowfield about fifty feet up-slope from the hole I had made, arriving at the other side without difficulty.

When I got to the landing site on the other side, Tim spotted me.

"Why the hell are you carrying a tree around with you?" he asked as I finally got my feet on dirt. I told him what had happened. Twenty minutes later the helicopter arrived. As we lifted off I looked back to see the spot where I had fallen. There was only a nondescript small hole in the snow perhaps a foot in diameter. Had I dropped out of sight into the crevasse, it would have been a long time before I was found.

"What a beautiful day," I said to Jim, as Tim, he and I walked to the helicopter. Jim nodded in agreement. It had been a few weeks since my fall through the snowfield.

"They don't get much better, that's for sure," he said.

Under a deep blue July sky, Cone Mountain stood over us, emerging from wispy fragments of night fog, a giant rising from a deep sleep. The yellow-gold rays of a rising sun lit the top of the peak from behind. Cool, still air promised a gentle, brilliant day. The mountain beckoned us to step out, to look up, to breathe deeply, offering its best to us in a friendly gesture.

When we reached the helicopter, Jim pulled out his map and asked, "Where's Randy sending you today?"

"We've finished with the local area, so we're starting regional reconnaissance today," I replied. "We'll fly up the north slope of the mountain to the Flat Spot and traverse our way north down this ridge line right here." I showed him the route on my copy of the map, while Jim copied it to his.

"Looks easy enough," he said. "Anything else?"

"Tim, you got anything?" I asked.

"Nope," Tim replied. "Ready to go."

"All right, let's load up," he said.

We had made the short flight to the Flat Spot many times. It was one of the few areas we could land the helicopter without toeing in, so we had used it while we sampled the northern slopes of the mountain. Situated above tree line, it was a seasonal snow-melt pond about thirty feet across that had gone dry. Small fragments of granite and packed sand covered the crusty bottom, providing us with a perfect landing pad.

As we approached for landing, a ptarmigan, perched on a nearby boulder, instinctively remained motionless despite the scream of the helicopter turbine and blast of the rotor wash. The poor bird, however, still had its brilliant white winter feathers, so it stood out from the tan and lichen-covered rocks like a flashlight in the dark.

Tim and I exited the helicopter and moved forward, squatting so Jim could see that we were clear. He lifted off to about twenty feet, pivoted, and in a rush of rotor wash nosed down the slope toward camp where he would ferry the next crew to their starting point. The roar dwindled, leaving us with the small sounds of morning birds and mosquitoes, and the motionless ptarmigan. We proceeded to organize our small backpacks. It was only when we stood up and swung them to our backs that the startled bird flew off in a rush of wings.

"All right," Tim drawled as we began walking north, "I been meanin' to talk to you about the current state of affairs with regard to who is field supervisor and who is field assistant on this team. I'm pretty sure I'm better qualified to be supervisor, because I'm taller than you."

"Hah! Yeah, I see your point," I replied, grinning, "but you see, as I am so much older—and therefore wiser—the Powers That Be have chosen me to lead. Perhaps, someday, when you grow up, you can be a field supervisor, too."

Tim snorted, laughing. "Now, that'd be one interpretation of your advanced years," he said, "but I'm thinkin' that perhaps you're a little too old for this job. When you get older, ya know, you get a little slower as you walk, kinda shaky sometimes, and obviously a little slower on the uptake, if ya know what I mean."

"Well, I hear you, but we've got some work to do now, so let's have a staff meeting at lunch to discuss the matter further. Agreed?"

"Hmmph," he replied, grinning back at me, "I guess it can wait that long."

We ambled down the ridge line at a leisurely pace, keeping an eye out for bears and enjoying the morning. The ridge was underlain with layered metamorphic rocks, ancient sediments of a Paleozoic ocean basin that had been buried hundreds of millions of years ago, then compressed by the movement of tectonic plates. Under intense pressure and high temperatures at depth, they deformed and folded, first becoming pliable, then oozing like hot, thick toothpaste. Buried deeply, over time they changed from what had been an unremarkable mud or sand layer into a sparkling schist, laced with gold-colored mica, clear quartz, and grayish feldspars. At times, small dark-red garnets were scattered in the matrix, like gleaming raisins in a layered cake.

As a result of the way the schists were oriented, lying in flat beds, they underlay the ridge line, not in a sharp, narrow crest, but as a series of gentle benches descending to the north. Each bench presented a flat area, gradually blooming with more heather, wildflowers, and stunted alder at lower and lower elevations, giving way to spruce and pine at tree line.

It was like walking a golf course, always downhill, surrounded by great shining mountains and blue-white glaciers. A cool, gentle breeze kept most of the mosquitoes away. We often heard the cutting screech of an eagle soaring overhead, or the ragged scrawk of a blackbird defending its territory.

At the first bench, I said, "Let's get our first sample here."

"Sounds good," Tim replied, and we sat down in a likely spot. Tim pulled a small shovel blade out of his pack, one designed to attach to our rock hammers, and proceeded to dig a hole in the dirt. I pulled out the sample tags and logbook to record the sample number, location and rock description. This was the extent of our separate roles. Field assistants did the digging, field supervisors wrote reports. In all other things we were equals, and over the season we had become best of friends.

As Tim dug, we talked. "What a beautiful place," Tim said. "We could be the first people to walk on this spot in thousands of years, maybe even ever!"

"Yeah," I replied. "It's astounding when you think about it." I hesitated, then went on. "But once in a while, something runs through my mind. This place is so beautiful, so special; if we found something, would we want to tell them? Are there places where there shouldn't be mines, and places where it's okay? What do you think?"

This was heresy. After all, we worked for a mining company.

"You know," Tim responded, "I've been thinking along the same lines. On one hand, we can't have a civilization without using raw materials. We need trees for our houses, metals for tools, for electricity, and petroleum to do just about everything else. We can't live without these things, it'd be like going back to the dark ages. Even the cave men were miners, 'cause they hunted for the best rocks for spear points and arrowheads and other stuff."

"Yeah, I agree," I said. "Yet nobody seems to have figured that out. It seems like you're either for or against the environment, regulations and such. There's no room for a middle ground. You're just considered a traitor to both sides if you say anything."

"Yeah," Tim said with a sigh. "Oh well. But hey, look around. Right now they're paying us to do this!"

I laughed, "They sure are!"

We packed up and headed down the slope, bench by bench, marveling at our luck and the beauty around us. At the end of the day, waiting for our ride, we sat in silence, looking out over the mountains, the grinding of glacial ice coming to us as low, rumbling echoes across the valley.

"This place is special," I said. "It needs a name."

135

We called it Thirteen Cup Ridge, after the number of samples we had collected.

We fervently hoped none of them detected a damn thing.

Two weeks later, the weather had turned. It was a gray day, windless and cold, with drizzle and hungry mosquitoes our constant companions.

The unnamed creek Randy had assigned us for reconnaissance sampling was about five miles long, and steep-sided along its entire length. It emptied into the Ketete River about ten miles downstream from camp. At that point we would need to find a place to ford the river and get to a suitable landing site.

Before Jim dropped us off, we slowly flew upstream along its length, checking for bears and moose. There was nothing but dense-packed alders and thorny devil's club.

We landed at the head of the valley, locating our position on the topographic map I carried. I made note of the geology, then we made our way downhill to the upper section of the drainage basin. We were able to get one or two sediment samples from side drainages before we reached tree line.

"That doesn't look like fun," I commented, as we stood contemplating our path. We were confronted with a wall of ragged, dripping green, a tangle of alders and brush, laced with skunk cabbage and devil's club that would hide anything—like a bear—more than twenty feet away. Worse, the walls of the canyon steepened as we dropped in elevation, offering no easy escape route.

"We'll be trapped in there," I said to Tim. "The walls are too steep and wet to climb out if we come up on a bear or moose."

"Yeah, this one looks bad," Tim replied. "I don't see any way around it, especially if we're gonna try to get some stream sediment samples. I'm thinkin' we need machetes instead of rock hammers."

"Yeah," I said with a sigh. "Let's make a lot of noise as we go, to scare off the bears, and stick close together. Ready?"

"As I'll ever be," Tim said. And with that, we dove into the Alaskan version of a jungle.

The first quarter mile wasn't bad, despite the soggy ground. It was like most young forests at this latitude, with trees and brush thin enough that you could make your way without too much trouble. Lower down, however, it got thicker. Thirsty mosquitoes, lying in wait for fresh blood to blunder into their domain, found us.

They swarmed over our heads, flying into our eyes and ears. No amount of bug spray halted their airborne attack. As the brush and trees got thicker and more difficult to traverse, they flew into our open mouths as we breathed harder with the effort, sticking to our tongues and the back of our throats, making us gag as we hastened to spit them out.

It got worse. The limbs of the densely packed alders formed an interwoven web that arched over the creek. The ground itself was swallowed up by the greenery, replaced by springy alder limbs. Forced to climb from limb to limb to make progress, we must have looked like drunk children on an insane, living jungle gym. We heard but could not see the swiftly running water in the creek below.

"Tim," I gasped. "We're not gonna get samples now. We gotta get out of this fuckin' creek as soon as we can. Let's just keep going."

Tim nodded, not wanting to open his mouth and let in the buzzing horde.

We didn't stop. We just kept climbing, slipping off the wet branches. Often our legs slipped between limbs and roots, sometimes going deep enough to hit the cold, fast water below.

Hell, even bears avoid this place, I thought.

An eternity of bugs and sweat and bruised ankles had passed when Tim, ahead of me, exclaimed "Oh my god, we made it!" I looked up to see, through the trees, an open, beautiful sand bar in the Katete River. A sand bar never looked so good. But we had one last hurdle. We had to ford the river to get to a place where Jim could land to pick us up.

The Katete ran deep at this point, with fast channels and eddies where the creek joined the river. We had no choice but to move either upstream or down to find a shallow area to cross. This meant following the river along its bank—through more alders and brush.

"Either way we go, it looks about the same to me," Tim said, holding onto an alder branch and hanging out over the river as far as he dared, peering up and down the stream.

"Well, the map shows a meander channel hugging the bank along here and further downstream," I replied, checking the topographic map. "But these channels change each year with the spring runoff."

"Okay, six of one, half dozen of the other. Which one, boss?" Tim said, grinning again.

"Why, upstream, of course." I replied quickly. "It's intuitively obvious to the casual observer!" We laughed in a sour sort of way.

Moving upriver three hundred yards took another hour. Eventually we came to a wide, shallow branch of the channel, a nice big gravel bar on the other side beckoning to us. We forded it easily, and gratefully settled down against a log to wait for our ride.

As we sat, exhausted, Tim turned to me, a mock-serious look on his face. "Now, about that supervisor's position."

That evening after dinner, we all sat on logs or in the sand looking out over the valley and the mountain above it, sipping our beer. Despite mosquitoes and crevasses, despite cold and isolation, I marveled at my good fortune. That small rock I discovered on the railroad tracks so long ago had led to a career promising a life-long series of adventures in exotic, far-flung places. Bush camps? Helicopters? They were my tools. Mountains? Glaciers? They were the matchless works of art on the walls of my office.

I had found the love of my life in Barb. I worried about her while I was gone as, I was sure, she worried about me. But we had a great and loving future ahead of us. The secret girl in me, the urge to put on a skirt or a dress, was contained again, only emerging rarely now. When I looked ahead, there was hope for the future.

But I kept my guard up. I had more to lose now than ever before.

TRANS-FORMATIONS

Twenty-One

Sheep Creek - 1978

The following summer the company hired me and the others again.

Another bush camp program, this one located about twenty-five miles east of Denali National Park on Sheep Creek in the Alaska Range Mountains. We were tasked with examining a copper-gold deposit to determine its potential, and to do some regional reconnaissance as well. It promised to be another summer in another beautiful place with a helicopter at our disposal.

The door to our tent flew open as my tentmate Abe and I sat talking.

"Rick!" Tim yelled, wide-eyed at the door. "Grab your camera!"

I jumped, snagged my camera from the plywood shelf next to my bunk, and followed Abe outside.

There before us, streaming through camp—past the parked helicopter, around the big kitchen tent, and onward past our throbbing generator was a herd of perhaps 150 caribou. Intent on their migration, they must have trudged doggedly up Sheep Creek, stopping for nothing. If an obstacle presented itself, they just flowed around it, heads down, panting as they raced southward, up and over the hills.

I began snapping pictures, one after the other, trying to keep caribou and helicopter in one shot, kitchen tent and caribou in another. They ignored us. In less than a minute they passed through our little camp and disappeared into the hills to the south.

We spent the next twenty minutes wandering around camp, looking for damage and picking up the caribou's calling cards with a shovel, dumping them in a nearby dry gully.

As I picked up poop scattered on the rocks, I paused to look up at the Alaska Range piercing the sky around me. Unlike the massive bulk of Cone Mountain and verdant valleys of southeast Alaska, Sheep Creek cut through ragged-edged blades of gray rock standing on end, slicing into the sky. We were well above tree line here, yet life was abundant amidst the loose grit and sharp stones.

"Shh," I whispered to Tim. "Let's go."

We walked toward a small bluff just fifty yards from camp, stepping carefully so as to make as little noise as possible as we crossed the rocky creek bed. On top of the bluff, perhaps thirty feet above the valley floor, lay a grassy, sunny meadow about the size of a basketball court. We crept up the sloping side of the rock-strewn hill.

Peering over the edge, two dozen brilliantly white Dall sheep, ewes and kids, scattered around the meadow enjoying the warm sun and fresh grass. They looked up at us, unafraid. They had grown used to our presence. They often stayed in place whenever we neared or made a commotion, barely curious even when the helicopter took off and landed. We had never ventured this close on foot before, however, not wanting to disturb them further.

I slowly pulled up the camera so as not to alarm them, braced it on a rock, and began snapping pictures. Some of the sheep slept, usually ewe and kid close together. Some played, the kids jumping and pretending to butt heads, while the ewes, teats and milk sacs evident, grazed nearby on the fresh grass. We watched in reverent silence for perhaps ten minutes. Then, with a shared glance and nod, we slid quietly back down the hill and walked away.

"Holy shit! That felt like the wind lifted our tent, floor and all!"

"Yeah, it sure did." Abe replied, eyes wide.

The warm Chinook winds had increased over a long, exhausting day on the mountain, howling down the slopes of the Alaska Range from the south, hurling grit into our eyes and at times and making it difficult to stand. We spent most of the day sheltering behind rock outcrops, chipping our samples. After dinner we all retired to our tents, hoping to rest.

I stepped to the plywood door and peered out. "The helicopter seems to be okay. Bill tied it down pretty good. We'd be screwed without it."

"Yes, that could be a problem." Abe replied, grinning. "We might run out of beer!"

Another great gust of wind tore through the air. Cutting over the howl, the sound of screeching nails pulling out of lumber could be heard, plywood and two-by-fours crashing to the ground. We rushed outside.

Off to our right, disaster. Bill's tent, the one most exposed to the wind, had been torn off its rock supports and thrown nearly thirty feet down the slope, landing on its side. The second tent, belonging to Tim and Dean, hung precariously off its supports, but remained upright.

The door to Bill's tent flopped open. He had been inside when it rolled.

"Damn!" He swore into the waning light. Standing in the doorway in his t-shirt and underwear, Bill had a trickle of blood running down the left side of his face.

"Bill, you okay?" I shouted.

"Yeah, just a scratch I think," he shouted back. "But give me a hand. I gotta get these tools and parts out of the tent and into a safe spot before this damn tent rolls again."

We scampered down the slope to his tent. Bill handed box after box through the door: tool box, packages of fuel and oil filters. Larry, the project geologist in charge, Tim and Dean rushed up behind us.

"Hey! Is everyone all right?" Larry yelled over the wind. We all nodded.

"Okay," he said, scanning the damage, his lips pressed hard together. The wind still buffeted us, making it difficult to stand. There was a risk of further destruction if we did not act quickly.

He turned to Dean. "Dean, grab all the rope you can find. We gotta tie down the tents, including these two. We have to make sure they don't get blown into the helicopter."

"Roger that," Dean said, and headed off toward the supply boxes on the other side of the big kitchen tent.

For the next hour, buffeted by the wind, we scrambled to secure the remaining tents and the pile of debris from Bill's tent. We ran out of rope and were forced to scavenge our water supply hose. We could do without water till morning.

Finally, we gathered bags of rock samples collected over the preceding weeks and piled them in the upwind corner of our kitchen tent. It was there we spent the night under the whipping canvas, rocks and sleepless geologists all huddled together in a miserable heap.

The next morning dawned with an eerie calm, the valley cloaked in thick fog. We walked through camp looking for stray trash while Bill and Larry took a careful look at the helicopter. It had survived the night, but our camp had not. Two tents of our four had been rendered unusable, the outhouse was destroyed, and we had no water. We could rebuild the camp, we knew, but more storms were coming.

Two days later we shut down the camp. We found lodging in a double-wide mobile home in nearby Healy. The nice elderly lady who owned the home still lived there. She wasn't wild about sharing her place with a gang of smelly, dirty geologists, but she was certainly happy about the unexpected income.

I squinted through the small hand lens at the rock I held close to my face, angling in a futile attempt to catch a bit more of the weak afternoon sunlight. It had been just over two weeks since our camp was destroyed by the wind. We were commuting to the worksites on the peaks by helicopter every day now.

I can't quite tell if it's pyrite or chalcopyrite, I thought. I need better light. Looking up, I caught sight of oddly bluish clouds to the south that clawed at the bottom edge of the sun. The wind, a gentle breeze that morning, had picked up again and whipped at us as we doggedly mapped the rocks and collected samples along the crest of the barren peak.

I looked over at Larry about fifty feet away. "Do you think the helicopter will be able to land?" I said in a loud voice.

"No, not up here," he replied looking around. "I think we're gonna have to move down the lee slope and find the best spot we can."

He signaled to Abe and Tim. We packed up our gear and samples, then started downhill. Even as we went, the wind tore at us as we picked our careful way down the rocky, barren slope: four staggering, overloaded hikers, Gore-Tex flapping in the wind.

We found a spot above tree line on the scree below the peak. There was no level ground available. We settled on an area clear of large boulders that wasn't so steep that the helicopter's blades would hit the ground as Bill did a toe-in. We all knew it was risky in such wind, but there was no alternative.

At about six o'clock the insistent throp-throp-throp of the helicopter faded in and out over the deeper, less regular moan of the wind. We spotted Bill as he came over the ridgeline west of us. The helicopter lurched and pivoted in the sky like a ping-pong ball as he fought to hold the aircraft on a steady course.

As he struggled to bring the egg-shaped craft lower to the ground, the wild motion appeared to slacken. He approached carefully, then touched the front of the skids to the ground. The rear of the skids hung unsteadily in the air about two feet off the ground.

I moved to a position where Bill and I could see each other. After a moment he glanced at me and nodded. I bent down, rock-filled pack in my hands, and moved toward the helicopter, ducking to be sure I cleared the whirling blades above my head. In this wind they flexed up and down as much as a foot as they spun.

I climbed carefully into the helicopter as Bill worked the stick and pedals to keep it on the ground. Sliding into the front center seat, I buckled into the harness and put on my headset, keying the mike.

"All set," I said. He nodded in reply.

I gave Larry the nod, then pushed well back in the seat so Bill could see. Just as Larry got both feet on the skid and was preparing to get in, an angry gust of wind came at us from underneath. The helicopter jumped about five feet into the air. Larry held on until Bill brought us carefully back to ground level. The last two geologists, Tim and Abe, were able to get into the back seats without incident.

When all reported "ready" over the intercom, Bill nodded and replied, "Here we go."

He lifted the helicopter straight up, gaining about twenty feet of altitude. As he did so, he pivoted us to the right. Abruptly, another fierce gust caught the helicopter from underneath. In a flash we found ourselves looking straight down at the ground just feet from the copter's nose as we hung from our harnesses. The wind seized us from behind and hurled us down the rocky slope.

No one spoke as we dangled, swept by the wind like a stray leaf in a fast-moving stream. In my head was an image of the small creek at the bottom of the slope and the steep embankment on the other side. If we slammed into it, rotor blades first, we would not survive.

Bill fought for control. Jammed against him in the cramped cabin, I could feel the muscles in his right leg and arm working to make adjustments to the controls. His knuckles were white as he clenched the stick between his knees.

We hung suspended in the turbulent air, crammed into our little bubble, nose down, waiting to see what the hurricane would do with us.

Bill pulled back on the stick. Slowly, the nose eased its way up. The horizon descended into our field of view, a strip of dirty gray sky appearing above the rocks. We could now see where the wind was pushing us. There, at the bottom of the hill less than a quarter of a mile away, stood the opposite bank of the creek. It was higher than we were, and getting close. I could pick out the spot where we would crash.

Bill saw it too. He stabbed the right pedal, pivoting the little helicopter to the right. At the same time he pulled the stick to the right, tilting us so the blades bit into the wind.

An endless, blurred moment later we streaked over the creek at about ten feet, turbine screaming, rotor blades slapping the air frantically. We cleared the wall of rock with only feet to spare.

Not yet done with us, the twenty-minute flight back to town continued the contest, a fight between the angry, howling wind and the screaming turbine of the little helicopter.

It's too soon, I thought, as we struggled through the whipping air. It's not fair. We just got started, Barb and I. We've got a future. If I die today, then what? Barb will go on, but she'll have to go through hell to do it. She'll have to clean up after me, go through pictures and things and clothes.

Oh shit. Clothes.

She'll find those old panty hose. She'll find that lipstick I pulled out of the trash. And her old bra. She'll find out about me in the worst possible way.

I know what I'm afraid of most right now. It isn't death.

It's discovery.

TRANS-FORMATIONS

Twenty-Two

Thomas Caldera - 1979

In May of 1979, I graduated from Oregon State University with a Master's Degree in Economic Geology. I was hired by the Uranium Division of the Anaconda Minerals Company in Denver, a highly regarded mining company that had been around since the 1880s. I could hardly believe my luck.

We moved to Denver, where Barb started school at the University of Colorado. Settling into a new house purchased with help from the GI Bill, we were happily on our way to middle-class normalcy.

"So, Rick, your first project is to produce a geologic map of the Thomas Caldera," said my new boss, Robert. He had been with Anaconda Minerals in Denver for more than twenty-five years, and was a well-known exploration geologist.

"It's just outside of Delta, Utah, and we think the volcanic rocks show the right chemistry to host a uranium deposit. If there's one there, it's up to you to find it."

"How long do I have?" I asked. I had visions of a week or two in the field.

"Oh, it'll take you several months, at least. The caldera is about twenty miles in diameter, possibly more. It's nearly the size of the Yellowstone Caldera, but older."

"Wow," I said.

"I'll join you on your first ten-day field cycle to get you going, and I'm available to help you all along the way. The first thing you need to do, however, is learn about the specific types of deposits you might find out there—we call them models—so you'll know what you're looking for." He pivoted to the credenza behind his desk, picking up a thick pile of reports and papers.

"Here. Study these," he said, turning back to me with a grin. "We leave for the field on Monday."

The glorious early morning sunshine beamed low over the Utah desert. A faint whiff of dew hung in the still, cool air under a limitless blue sky.

I'm finally a full-time geologist, I thought, as I cruised down the long, straight gravel road. I'm doing geology. I'm getting paid to do geology. I've got a truck and tools and an expense account to go out and do geology. I have a real job, doing nothing but geology!

I grinned like an idiot at the endless desert, profoundly happy as the sagebrush whipped by.

I had spent an intense ten-day field cycle with Robert, learning to use stereographic air photos and satellite imagery with topographic maps as the basis for my exploration work.

The basic process was simple. Start in an area that was easy to access. Precisely locate yourself on the topo map. Log the geology at that point, then use the air photos to track that rock formation from where you are, as far as possible. When you reach a point where the geology appears to change or some other feature obscures the rocks, go there. Figure out the geology at that point, then move on in the same way, always watching for signs of mineralization in the rocks. It was like assembling a massive jigsaw puzzle miles across, each piece a challenge, a multi-dimensional mystery to be solved before you moved on to the next.

This empty bit of desert and mountains were mine to figure out. Not another living soul for miles. Just me, my hammer, a hand lens and some maps and photos.

My first stop was a small valley in the Drum Mountains, a range of peaks that bordered the caldera. They consisted of a thick sequence of sedimentary rocks: quartzites, shales, and dolomites, most from the Devonian Period more than 400 million years ago. The adjacent peaks of the Thomas Range to the north consisted of volcanic rhyolites that had been dated to less than 50 million years old in the Tertiary period. My task was to map out the contact between the two, if possible, and see if there were any ore deposits hiding there.

Two weeks later, I sat on the hot cab of my truck, feet dangling over the back window, peering through my small field binoculars at an outcrop perhaps a mile away across the desert.

I had parked on the side of the gravel road stretching through the sagebrush near an area that had looked a bit odd on the air photos. The color and texture of the rocks on either side of a small gully had visibly changed.

Putting away my binoculars, I hoisted my field pack to my back, and with rock hammer in hand stepped out across the desert at a leisurely pace.

As I moved, the fragrance of sagebrush was heavy in the air. It had a velvety sort of richness to it, but was underlain by the harder, acidic glint of sand and rock baking in the mid-afternoon sun. Far out over the hills, two vultures slowly circled. The only sound to be heard was the crunching of my boots in the gritty sand.

Slowly, the outcrop resolved itself as I approached. The left side, a dark, dirty gray, seemed layered, with beds tilted at a sharp angle. The right side was a light, ragged-looking gray, with the texture of a sponge.

It was clearly the contact between Devonian dolomites and Tertiary volcanics of the caldera. It has to be the ring fracture, I realized, the enormous fault zone that circles the entire twenty-plus mile caldera rim. I quickened my pace.

The fault contact between the two rock formations was thin as a pencil line. It traced its way vertically from top to bottom of the outcrop. Stepping forward, I placed my right hand against the fault, thumb on the sedimentary rocks, little finger on the volcanic rocks.

There, across that knife-edged contact was a time span of more than three hundred million years, a span that connected the remains of ancient shallow oceans crawling with bizarre, primitive creatures to a cataclysmic volcanic eruption tens of miles in diameter. That thin line spoke of planetary-scale power and deep, deep time.

I straightened up and looked around. I'm there again, I thought. I'm back on those railroad tracks on that hot summer day, looking for the next shiny rock, the next big discovery. This time, though, instead of a little piece of mica schist, I'm putting my hand on the edges of vastly different worlds, across unfathomable time.

I stood for a long moment, awestruck at what the little outcrop revealed and my good fortune to see and understand it. Finally, stepping back, I dropped my pack and pulled out my field notebook.

It was time to do some geology.

The heavy wooden door squealed as I pushed it open. I paused to let my eyes adjust, then stepped into the dim cavern of the Wagon Wheel Bar and Grill. It was the only place in town where I could get a beer with dinner. Sadly, it was a weak, thin, 3.2% Mormon beer.

"Hi Josh," I said as my eyes adjusted to the gloom. "Burger and fries and a Bud tonight."

"Roger that, Rick. Find any gold today?"

"Not a lick, Josh. Just sagebrush, rattlesnakes, and rocks out there." He knew I was not there to find gold. I had told him, long ago, that I was in the uranium business. It didn't matter.

"Aww, tough luck. Better next time, right?"

"Always next time, Josh. You got that right."

I moved to the table where I usually sat, next to the wall under the mounted head of a glassy-eyed antelope. I slid into a chair, ignoring the split reddish vinyl of the seat cover. The smell of grease emanated from the kitchen, and I could see movement back there, the flash of a hand as it lifted order tickets from the pass-through window. The cook had never emerged from behind the wall in the month I had frequented the place. It was as if a shadow immersed in a cloud of hot grease had made my burgers.

Josh came from around the bar and set a bottle of beer in front of me, no coaster or glass. The bottle gleamed brown in the dim light, beads of yellowish sweat on it. Like the color of piss, I thought for a moment, then put the cold bottle to my mouth and took a deep, long swig.

The Wagon Wheel Bar and Grill was a farmer's and rancher's place. Hooks on the wall, made from deer and elk antlers, were distributed around the room, each a suitable location for the preservation of the curl on your Stetson. The locals allowed me—a Stetsonless interloper—into the establishment because they hoped I might find gold or uranium or whatever on their property. Then they could retire to Arizona or Idaho, or even godless Florida to live out their days playing golf or fishing all day, not herding stinking cattle or growing alfalfa.

We all have our dreams, I thought. Even here.

Someone dropped a few quarters in the juke box, and the angry wail of country music filled the dark room. "Take This Job and Shove It," the singer growled. Minding my own business, I went to work on my burger and fries when they appeared, then ordered another beer. Only lightweights and faggots drank just one beer at the Wagon Wheel. A few more ranchers came in as I ate, but I didn't know them. They knew about me, of course, and nodded in my direction. I nodded back. Yes, I was considered acceptable, more or less.

"What do I owe ya, Josh?" I finally asked as I stood up and stepped back to the bar.

"That'll be $8.50 all in," he replied, as he dug out pickled pigs feet from a huge jar on the bar for another customer.

I dropped a ten dollar bill on the counter. "Keep the change."

"Thanks, Rick. See ya next time. Bring me a nugget, will ya?"

"Just as soon as I find one," I replied.

I stepped out the squeaky front door of the Wagon Wheel and into the early Utah evening.

The sunset over the mountains west of town lent an orange-red glow to the air, even as the sky to the east faded from lavender to purple. I stood for a moment, taking it in. Then, looking both ways down the empty highway that was the main street of town, I ambled across the road to the small motel that was my temporary home.

Once inside, I carefully closed the curtains, being sure there were no gaps. I sat down at the round table near the window, pulled off my boots, dropping them to the floor. Crossing the room, I stepped out of my jeans, shirt and underwear and padded into the bathroom for a quick shower.

My suitcase was spread open on a rack just outside the bathroom door. Emerging from the bathroom, I dug into the bottom of the case until I found my cloth laundry bag. In it were the stretched-out bra that Barb had thrown away, an ancient pair of panty hose once intended for polishing boots, and an old tube of lipstick, nearly used up.

I slipped the bra around my waist, fastening it, then pulled it up over my shoulders. Using a pair of clean socks, I put one in each cup, wadding them up. Sitting on the bed, I rolled the panty hose over my feet and up my legs. The hose were stretched out from years of use. I could pull them up over my torso to ride just under the bra if I wanted, but I just folded them over at my waist.

Back in the bathroom, I added just a touch of lipstick to my lips, then took a hand towel and folded it around my head like a scarf.

Checking again to be sure the curtains were completely closed, I walked over to the television and turned it on, then went back to the bed. I pulled out the pillows and placed them against the headboard and sat down, leaning back.

While I watched television, I made notes in my day planner for my weekly report. Once in a while I stopped, closed my eyes, and leaned my head back. I breathed, feeling the bra, the hose, the touch of the towel on my ears and neck, relishing the moment. No longer a grubby, dirty male field geologist, sweaty and hot from a day's work, I was me, just me, wearing a used brassiere of my wife's and panty hose from a previous decade.

It was a peace, of sorts.

Most of the time I had no problem being one of the guys, doing the things that were expected of me. I enjoyed the subtle privileges of a white male professional. I was even accepted at the Wagon Wheel. But there was always an instinctive sense of caution. I still had to analyze all that I did, how I did it or said it, always careful not to give myself away. In a sense it was an act, being Rick, an act I had to perform every waking moment of every waking day.

Often I couldn't wait to get back to my hotel room and put on these pitiful things. I rated the rooms I stayed in by how well the curtains covered the windows and how large the mirrors were.

I agonized over this twisted side of me. In a way it was being untruthful to Barb, perhaps even unfaithful. I had hoped this part of me would dwindle, would fade to a distant memory. But it hadn't. I lived in a secret limbo, somewhere between male and female, between perversion and respectability.

I rationalized it, of course. It's just me, I would say to myself. I'm not hurting anyone. I'm still a husband, a geologist, and I love my wife. Really, I'm not hurting anyone.

SEDIMENTARY

"Are you sure about that?"the other voice would ask. "All this hiding, this subterfuge of a life, isn't it possible it's hurting someone?"

I dared not follow that line of thinking, sensing the answer I would find.

Eventually, I turned off the television and went to the bathroom, remembering to wipe off the lipstick. Back in bed, I switched off the light and rolled over on my side. I closed my eyes and waited for sleep to come, trying not to think. But in the ghostly shadow just before sleep, a wisp of thought, an unbidden vision came to me.

A vision of me—as her—walking in the sun, skirt swirling around my legs, as if I actually had the right to exist.

TRANS-FORMATIONS

Twenty-Three

Western Australia - 1982

The yellow-white heat of the Australian Outback sun glared down on the countryside around me as I drove, beating it into submission, beating it to a flat and blood-red frying pan of dust and scrub.

I had been transferred to Anaconda's International Division after my assignments in the western U.S. and Alaska. Along the way, they had also sent me to the jungles of Suriname, holding out the promise of a tour in Australia as bait. I went for it.

I made two trips to Suriname to arrange planning and logistics for a reconnaissance program in the western part of the country. Then came a bloody coup. It was not bad news to me when I was told Anaconda had shut down the program.

Thus I found myself in Western Australia. It was another camping situation, but without a helicopter. Our "billabong" bush camp was a two-and-a-half hour drive from the nearest civilization, a sad little truck stop on the desolate highway from Perth to Canarvon.

Let's see, I calculated, as I drove down the long, straight road. It's Sunday morning here. When I call Barb back in Denver it will be Saturday evening there. Hopefully the pay phone at the truck stop is working this time.

My little Toyota truck was humming along, a blood-red dust plume roiling out behind me. I had settled in for the long haul when suddenly three emu exploded from the desert to my right and began running. The long-legged birds stayed together in a smooth, gliding pace parallel to the road, glancing anxiously at me as if I were some strange mechanical predator.

Gradually I slowed, coming to a stop and turning off the engine. The emu had stopped as well, standing together about one hundred yards away, nervous but curious.

I decided to try a little experiment.

I inserted a cassette into the player in the dashboard and turned up the volume. The opening melodies of Beethoven's Sixth Symphony, the Pastoral, danced from the speakers. I increased the volume, then sat back, camera in hand.

The emu, still staring, began tilting their heads, first to one side then the other, as they tried to decipher the strange sound emanating from this metal creature crossing their desert. After a minute, one took a step closer. The second followed, then the third. I raised the camera slowly, so as not to alarm them, got them in the frame and in focus, and began taking pictures.

For about fifteen minutes, I rationed my shots as the emu inched closer, coming within a few feet of the truck. There they stayed, heads tilting one way, then another, even as the brass section bellowed and timpani boomed in the thunderstorm movement. Suddenly, one stepped to the front of the vehicle and in a blur of motion, pecked the hood. *Whack!*

162

It occurred to me that perhaps I should be more careful here. I put down the camera and leaned over to close the passenger side window. The emu were startled by my movement, and in a flurry of feathers and red dust, all three bounded back to the safety of the desert.

I watched after them as they quickly disappeared into the scrub, wishing Barb had been here to see them with me.

I learned a new phrase while working in the Outback. "The Tyranny of Distance," they called it. Everything was far away, no matter where you needed to go. Want to go to town? Five hours round trip. Be sure to take extra gas and water. Have to attend a meeting at the home office in Perth? Half a day to the airport, and a two-hour flight later you're sitting at the conference table already tired. Even the property we were working on, Uaroo Station, was huge, covering 500,000 hectares, or about 1.3 million acres.

But there were other distances more immediate to me, measured not in distance, but in time. It had been five months away from Barb, and it had been more than five months since I had dressed.

I called Barb in Denver almost every Sunday while in the field. It was a cherished privilege, even though at times it was painful that I could not reach out and touch her, be with her. She would tell me about her classes at the university and all the day-to-day aspects of home life that I missed. But such things were a universe away from my tent at Uaroo Station. I couldn't help her, she couldn't help me.

She was having a hard time with our separation, too.

I dared not carry any women's clothes with me when I travelled internationally. The risk of a customs agent checking my baggage at the airport was too great, and there were very few dressing opportunities in a bush camp. So I steadfastly warned myself to man up, to do my job, to love my wife.

Of course, it made little difference.

In my daydreams in the field, in the dark desert nights in my tent, I thought often of Barb. But I also dreamed of wearing a dress. One moment I'd be thinking of the next day's mapping, or geochemical samples, or the supplies we needed, the next of wearing a blue flowered skirt and complementary top while at dinner with a friend.

Was I just obsessed? I didn't think so, at least in the way I understood obsession. No, it was simply in the background. It was a ready place to go when my mind wandered, always there for me. A seductive, comfortable place.

No one suspected. I was respected by my crew, and I respected them. I worked with them, supervised them in the field, and drank beer with them no differently than any other "Yank" they'd met before. That went for my colleagues back in the States. No different. Just the same: always, constantly, ever carefully, the same.

Yet things were changing rapidly back in the States. By the time I returned, Anaconda had shut down the entire uranium division. Three Mile Island had effectively ended the construction of new nuclear power plants in the United States, thus diminishing the demand for uranium.

I was lucky. The International Metals division took me on just as they had my former boss, Greg. He had become manager of Arco Minerals Norway.

Arco Oil & Gas owned Anaconda. Arco wanted a piece of the action in the oil fields of the North Sea, and the Norwegian government looked kindly on other kinds of investment by the big oil companies.

That investment was us.

TRANS-FORMATIONS

Twenty-Four

Old Mud Puddles - 1984

It was called the Rombak project. It was yet another bush camp, this one situated on a high plateau outside of Narvik on the Norwegian coast near the Arctic Circle. A small lead-zinc-silver outcrop had been discovered there, and we were tasked with finding more, if possible.

The plateau was a barren pile of slick, lichen-covered rocks and soggy muskeg swamps two thousand feet above sea level. Swept by storms racing in from the North Sea, it was always near freezing or below, always wet, always gray.

We lived in small backpack tents, and there was no way to get warm or dry. Mud was everywhere, which we couldn't help but track into our tents. Clothes, sleeping bags—everything developed an ever-present, moist dankness. We washed ourselves in snow-melt ponds, often frozen over with a thin film of ice. There was no cook, thus we shared the cooking duty on a rotation. Meal quality varied accordingly.

Our toilet was a hard plastic milk crate with the bottom broken out. As we sat perched over a deep crack in the rocks, our lowered underwear filled with sleet or snow if we didn't hunch over. The toilet paper was kept in a coffee can at our feet, which we had to use quickly before it got too wet. Many mornings as I sat, I yearned for the luxurious good old days in Alaska when we had a real toilet with a seat, a shower, and a dry place to sleep.

My crew, all Norwegian and Danish grad students, were all on tight budgets and had to provide their own food. Thus, most of the time we ate out of cans. Canned potatoes, boiled. Perhaps a canned vegetable. But, worst of all, canned fish balls.

Fish balls, a Norwegian staple, consisted of ground white fish meal shaped like an egg-sized ball. There was little we could do to make them taste better, so usually they were served with a simple white sauce. I had an expense account, however, so once a week I went into town via helicopter for our weekly mail and food run. At the market in Narvik I purchased a supply of meat, fruit, and fresh vegetables for the camp—anything that was not fish balls.

But I could do nothing about either the weather or the rocks—those slippery, twisted, endlessly boring, indistinguishable rocks.

"Hallo!" I shouted into the fog.

"Ja, Hallo!" was the reply through the mist. "Ve are on line 0700 at 050. Okay?"

"Ja—uh, yes, that's good!" I yelled back. "I'm behind you at marker 010."

We had painstakingly laid out a grid over the project area using compass and surveyor's string. It was based on distance from a known location point, but we didn't know precisely where that was on the topo map. It was just a pile of rocks we built. We called it "Zero Point" and we measured from there. Once in place, we followed the string along the ground, taking samples at regular intervals. I crawled behind the sampling team, mapping the rocks.

Today, two of my crew were forty meters ahead of me taking rock chip samples. They were just voices in the fog, accompanied by the tink-tink-tink ring of their hammers on the outcrops.

Oddly, it was comforting to know they were close by. I had once tried working on another part of the plateau alone, but it clearly became apparent that that was a bad idea. Had I been hurt, finding me quickly would have been impossible.

And the rocks? I hated those rocks. Hated 'em. Map them? Hell, the whole damn plateau was a sequence of sediments— claystones, mudstones, fine-grained sandstones, all in repetitive thin layers no thicker than an inch. They were all the same. No difference. There was no unique layer that could be traced for any distance so I could get a handle on the folding or faulting or any damn thing.

The plateau was more than twenty square miles of Precambrian dried-up mud puddle turned on its side and squeezed like toothpaste. Lead-zinc-silver deposit? There was one little outcrop about the size of a bathtub. The rest was shit. All shit.

There was one bright spot at Camp Rombak. For communications, we had a radio telephone.

It was a maritime band radio, used by the local fishing boats and other craft at sea. We called the operator in Narvik, gave her the number, and she connected us to the outside world via the Norwegian telephone system.

About three months into the program, I determined to call Barb in Denver. I didn't care what it cost.

As I had been practicing my Norwegian for several months, I thought that, although primitive, I had made sufficient progress to make a phone call. Surrounded by my crew one miserable evening after we had finished our fish balls, I keyed the microphone.

"Marine operatør, dette er Rombak camp." (Rombak camp calling).

"Ja, Rombak camp, mottar deg." (Receiving you).

"Vennligst koble til dette nummeret." (Please connect to this number).

"Ja, bare gå." (Yes, go ahead).

"Tre ni tre fire åtte." (Three nine three four eight.)

"Gjenta vennligst Rombak." (Repeat please, Rombak).

"Tre ni tre fire åtte." (Three nine three four eight.)

There was a long pause, then the reply:

"Ah, Rombak! English will be better for you!"

The crew exploded in peals of laughter. I stood, microphone in hand, feeling the warm glow of embarrassment creep up my face while they rocked back and forth, tears streaming from their eyes. Hundreds of people on the network had heard this exchange.

I keyed the mike.

"Thank you, operator."

"Iss not a problem, Rombak. Please hold."

Barb and I had a limited, very public conversation. In English.

Then one fine day, a miracle—the sun came out.

It was low on the northeast horizon, casting an eerie yellow-gold glow across the plateau through ragged clouds. The wet rocks gleamed in reflected glory, like rounded lumps of pale yellow diamond in the sun. The cool air was alive, fresh and clean, almost sweet. It was nearly solstice, and wonder of wonders the clouds had thinned and broken apart for the occasion.

Solstice. It was time to celebrate in the ancient Norwegian tradition.

I had been told the tradition called for a bonfire. There were no trees on the plateau, thus no firewood, except for the five artificial fireplace logs I had been able to buy in town and smuggle into camp in a nondescript cardboard box. The box also held three bottles of whisky and a package of red plastic beer cups.

"Okay guys, I've got an announcement. We're taking tomorrow off. Tonight after dinner we will celebrate the solstice and the good weather. Meet me down by the lower pond after you've cleaned up in here. Forstår du?"

"Ja! Ve understand!" was the enthusiastic reply.

I stepped out of the teepee and headed to our supplies, a pile of boxes covered with a big blue tarp, and pulled out the box of solstice cheer. Holding it to my chest, I hustled down the slope through soggy moss and over slippery rocks to the designated spot. It was a level area next to a large, clear pond of snow melt, one of hundreds of such ponds on the plateau. This one opened to the north, so that at midnight, if the weather cooperated, we might see the sun. We were located just sixty miles south of the Arctic Circle, thus most of the sun's disc would be above the horizon.

The crew finished cleaning the dishes and securing our food and assembled at the pond.

"Okay guys, here we go!" I opened the box with a flourish, and began handing out the logs.

"Build the bonfire right over there. And by the way...," I paused dramatically, then pulled out two of the bottles. "We've got something else to keep us warm!"

I passed out the beer cups and began pouring while they got the fire going. We stood around as the fire crackled and smoked to life.

Raising our cups, we toasted. "Lykkelig Sankthansaften!" they said.

"Huh?" I said.

The evening deteriorated from there. At one point I tried to teach them a song—Yes We Have No Bananas—in Norwegian, hopelessly trying to explain why we Americans wanted to sing about bananas we didn't have.

"Ja, vi har ingen bananer, Vi har ingen bananer i dag!"

Our ragged, off-pitch voices rang over the plateau, the sound bouncing from rock to rock, icy pond to frozen puddle, across the soggy moss and mud. We laughed till we cried, basking in the pale yellow light of the arctic sun and the warmth of our little bonfire.

We were still on the plateau in September. The weather, which had hampered us all "summer," got worse, covering the rocks with snow, making our survey lines invisible. It was time to quit.

A week before we began to close up shop, I received a small package in the mail. It was an award from the company for being a "Valued Employee" for five years—a clear glass paperweight with the Arco company logo etched into it.

Those HR types back in Denver ought to bring their asses up here to see what "Valued Employee" means, I groused. A paperweight? Is that what they think I do, push papers?

Two days before we flew out for good, I received more mail from my friendly HR department: my lay-off notice. I was to be unemployed as of November 1st, 1984. Anaconda Minerals, Inc. was to be dismantled, all properties sold to the highest bidder except the coal division, which would be folded into the Arco organization. Grand old Anaconda, which had been in operation since 1881, was suddenly gone.

On our last day, the snow and rain paused for a few hours. Camp was packed up and ready for transport in the helicopter. As we were waiting for it to arrive, I walked down the hill to our Solstice pond. I paused for a moment, looking at the ring of rocks where our bonfire had been, thinking of what we had been through those long, cold months.

I turned to the pond.

Leaning far back, I heaved my "Valued Employee" award high over the pond. It fell in a long, steep arc toward the thin ice of the newly frozen Norwegian water, making a satisfying "thunk-splash" when it broke through.

TRANS-FORMATIONS

Twenty-Five

Semi-Yankee - 1985

"What's an outlet mall?" I asked.

It had been six months since Anaconda folded. Luckily, I had found another job exploring for gold deposits in the southeastern U.S. with the FMC Gold Company, based in Denver.

"You ain't from 'round here, are ya," was the reply.

Earl was a tall, lanky man wearing dirty jeans and a tee-shirt with "Tarheels" emblazoned in big blue letters. He was the owner of a small farm near Burlington, North Carolina, where I had stopped to ask permission to collect a stream sediment sample on his land.

"Nossir, I'm from Missouri," I said. "We've got a family farm down on the Missouri River east of Kansas City."

I had learned that Missouri was an acceptable place to be from in those parts, as opposed to, say, New York or California, and I sometimes brought it up to show I weren't no damn Yankee.

"The company I work for is based in Denver, so I live there now."

"And you wanna prospect on my place lookin' for gold? I got that right?"

"Yessir, that's right. The first gold ever found in the U.S. was discovered just east of Charlotte. The belt of rocks that carries the gold comes this way and goes all the way to northern Alabama. I'm lookin' along that belt for a new deposit, and your place is right in the middle of it all."

"Well, hell, I sure wouldn't mind if you found gold on my place. You go ahead, but ya gotta tell me if you find anything. Okay?"

"Yessir, I sure will. And if there's gold here, we'll be back knockin' on your door with a contract offer soon enough. Thanks!"

We shook hands, and I turned back to my truck parked in the driveway of his double-wide mobile home. It was an old home, sad and in need of attention.

It's a hard life here, too, I thought.

There was a stand of corn next to the house, dry and rustling in the light breeze. It looked like he might have peanuts out back, or maybe soybeans. Perhaps he has a pot patch in the nearby woods, or a still, I thought. But he's letting me go out there, so probably not. It's one thing for me to speak the language, but quite another to be trusted with information like that.

After all, I ain't from around here.

I pulled off the highway and parked in the huge parking lot of a long strip mall. The only shade came from the huge sign that towered over the lot. Many cars were clustered there, trying to avoid the blazing North Carolina sun. I stepped out into the damp heat and bee-lined for the nearest store.

Jeez, this stuff is cheap, I noted as I wandered through the store aisles. Ten bucks for a dress shirt? That's pretty good. And look at that, fifteen bucks for a pair of jeans. I think I'm going spend some money in here.

I wandered around, aisle by aisle. I turned a corner and suddenly, looking up, I was confronted by a mannequin standing on a small platform at the end of a row. The dress it wore hit me like a brick—a shirtdress, royal blue in a flowing crinkled fabric, a wide tan belt of braided hemp with a modest buckle accentuating the waistline.

The thought came in a flash. It's like the dress I wore in Karen's basement. I'd look good in that dress....

I turned back into the men's section, but it was too late. My mind continued to race down a familiar path, rationalizing it, planning it, envisioning it, all in a split second.

Do it. Buy the dress. If you buy some men's clothes at the same time, the sales girls will think you're buying the dress for your wife. Just flash your wedding ring, fool. Maybe ask a stupid question about sizes. Pick a girl that's about Barb's size, or make a comment that she's a size 16 too. That is your size, isn't it, pervert? Isn't it? How about a bra? If you had any balls, you'd buy a bra or two. Do it. This is your chance. Do it. Just fucking do it.

"That'll be $95.45." the teenage sales girl said in a laconic, nasal voice. She was clearly bored to tears and couldn't care less what the customers did. I pulled my billfold out of my hip pocket, and counted out five twenties. I didn't use a credit card—that might lead to questions if Barb saw the charge on our account.

"Thanks," I said, and walked out with a large plastic bag of new clothes—two shirts, one pair of slacks, a blue crinkle shirtdress, and a two-pack of bras, size 42B.

It was a cheap vinyl case, swag from Irish Aer Lingus airlines that I found at a garage sale. Emerald green in color and the size and shape of a small briefcase, the airline logo was printed on both sides in white. In this, I began to accumulate my own clothes.

Over the next four years I accumulated more items, becoming ever bolder: first cosmetics, then panty hose and a simple knit skirt. Finally I summoned the courage to walk into a beauty supply store and purchase a wig.

I established a pattern. At the end of a sweaty day, a day filled with dirt and rocks and long hikes, I picked up dinner at a fast-food drive-thru on the way back to my motel. I'd take a quick shower, dress, then eat, and drink, while watching television.

I felt comfort in that act, but also shame. I could think of no easy answers, no way out. I could only continue hiding from everyone—including myself.

Twenty-Six

South Mountain - 1989

I did it again last night, dammit.

My head was pounding as I droned down the dusty desert road in my pickup truck under the glare of a yellow-bright morning sun. Drunk again, I had pulled out my Aer Lingus case with its collection of women's things and dressed. And drank. Why the hell can't I stop this, I asked myself? I sure deserve the hangover this time.

The exploration program in Georgia and the Carolinas had not produced any deposits of interest, so I was transferred to work in the western states. My new exploration area took me into the mountains and deserts of Oregon, Idaho, Montana, and Utah. They were easier places to explore, with better access, more outcrop, and greater geological potential for significant gold deposits.

The latest motel room smelled of disinfectant and old cigarettes, but it was the only motel in Jordan Valley, Oregon, the town nearest to my current operating area. I was following up on surface features I had targeted using satellite imagery. Most were on the Idaho side of the state line. As usual, I collected rock and stream sediment samples at specific locations I had noted on the map, while along the way watching for the characteristic signs of silver and gold deposits of the types that occurred in similar rocks—the twentieth-century version of a prospector.

I continued my pattern. Work all day, get food on the way home, shower, dress, drink. Then all I had to do was look into the mirror and there she was, the girl behind my eyes. That girl was me, and she was getting desperate. Ever since the outlet mall in North Carolina, she wanted out.

I slowed the truck, checking the topographic map in the seat next to me. Okay, I thought, A few miles more. Then I can hike cross-country to that deep-cut creek bed and grab a stream sediment sample. There's sure to be a decent outcrop for mapping and rock samples.

I pulled off the road a few minutes later, crossing a shallow ditch and parking in the shade of a large piñon tree. The air photo had shown that the piñon forest was dense here, so I needed to navigate my way to the site with my compass and topo map.

I parked, stepped out, and walked to the back to get my gear: leather belt with rock hammer and compass hanging in holders; orange field vest with pens, bags for samples, and the topo map tucked into an inside pocket, and finally my large field pack, empty except for small emergency kit, lunch, and a full water bottle. I jammed on my ratty old Vietnam jungle hat with the wide brim to shade my ears and eyes from the sun.

Checking my compass, I oriented myself, then looked to the horizon for a landmark. Most of my view was obscured by the tall piñon, but off to my right was the top of South Mountain, about six miles away. If I kept the peak at about forty-five degrees to my direction of travel, I'd be able to intercept the creek about where I wanted.

I trudged along, looking down at the sand and rocks at my feet, head still pounding from the hangover, weaving myself through the trees and low, dry brush.

The same old tape unspooled in my brain as I walked:

I gotta stop it, somehow. If I go to a shrink, and I don't tell Barb, she'll know something is going on. She'll think I'm having an affair or something. If I do tell her I'm seeing a shrink, she will want to know why or she will believe it's her fault and think I want to leave her.

No, I love her too much for that.

Anyway, how would I find the right psychologist, one that I can spill my guts to, one I can trust? I can't just "shop around." Can I trust anyone with this? If I'm just another pervert, a queer, then what about the rest of who I am? Does that matter at all? Do I have any right to be alive if all else is tainted by this damned, stinking urge? And if I am discovered, will I lose everything? What about Barb and Mom? What would happen to them?

"Yes, asshole," the voice in my brain whispered. "You will lose everything, and you will destroy their lives as well. Barb will leave you. Your mother will look at what she has birthed in utter horror, and turn her back. You'll be fired, never to work in geology again. If you're lucky, you'll be able to find a job flipping burgers. Under the bridge with you, pervert. That's your future if you screw up and let her out."

I jerked my head up just in time to see a tree branch at face level. I had nearly walked into it. I stopped, gazing off to my right toward South Mountain, staring at it for a long moment. I was a little off track, but not enough to matter. I skirted the tree in front of me and moved on, plodding. It felt like a thick, bad dream.

I focused on the rocks at my feet as I hiked onward, trying to think only of the job at hand. Trudging up the long, gentle slope, the rocks began to change from angular fragments of light colored rhyolite to dark, chunky pieces of black basalt. The slope was capped by an old basalt flow, it appeared. The basalt was more resistant to weathering, and thus covered the more prospective rocks underneath. If the creek bed was deep enough, however, it might cut through the basalt layers and expose the rhyolites again in just the right area.

I came to another dense stand of piñon. Turning sideways, I pushed my way through the tree branches, easing my way. Suddenly, my right foot slipped into nothingness. I grabbed at the branches. Pulling my foot back, I forced them aside to see where I had stepped.

It wasn't a hole I had stepped in. It was the edge of a cliff. I had arrived at the creek. The sides were not sloped as I had expected, but near-vertical walls perhaps one hundred feet high. At the bottom of the cliff were many large boulders of basalt that had broken from the cliff under my feet. Beneath them, the floor of the gorge revealed light-colored rhyolite.

I considered the situation. Okay, I can't get down there. It's too steep. It'd be dangerous if I tried to make my way down. I'm not here to practice my rock climbing skills, especially not alone.

Suddenly, exploding into my brain, it came to me—here was my chance.

"No one need ever know what a worthless piece of shit you are," whispered the acid voice in my head. "Right here, right now. You could end it all, make it go away. Just make it look like an accident, make it look like you decided to climb down the cliff on your own and fell, or like you were cutting through the trees and didn't see the edge.

"They won't find you for days, so you'd better do it right. Don't want to lie there with a broken back, dying slow. Hit head-first. Make it quick. Don't linger in pain. Here's your chance. This time it's for real. Here it is. Here.

"NOW."

Motionless in the desert heat, I balanced at the edge of the cliff.

"Just a twitch, a brief, sudden impulse," the voice persisted. "Drop your rock hammer over by that chunk of basalt. The search party will find it, as if you lost it when you fell. Scrape your foot along the rocks so they will think you scrambled for footing. Barb will get the insurance, and no one will find out about you. It'll fi-nally be over."

The turpentine fragrance of the piñon trees around me waft-ed through the heated desert air, mixed with the gritty smell of hot sand and rocks beneath my feet. Sweat trickled down my back under my pack. I could hear the faint sounds of insects, hopping and buzzing and crawling in their blind, incessant way. I lifted my head to look skyward through sticky eyes, swollen from crying.

Why? I silently asked for the millionth time. Why am I this way?

But the cloudless blue void above me had nothing to say on the matter. The rocks at my feet too were silent, their view of things focused on millennia, not moments, certainly not on mere human concerns.

Okay. This time it's real. This is no call for help. There's no one to help me. Not here, not back in the world. This is the point where I make my decision.

So. What are you gonna do, pervert?

I stood for an eternity, a lifetime. Then I backed out of the tree branches, turned, and walked to a boulder. I took off my pack and sat down.

I didn't want to die.

Besides, I soon realized, there was one little problem with the plan—my clothes were back in the motel room. My women's clothes and makeup and jewelry were there, stashed in my little green case. When I came up missing, they'd investigate, looking for clues as to where I had gone. They'd go through my stuff and find the clothes. I'd be exposed. They'd come to the conclusion it was suicide because I'm a pervert, and Barb wouldn't get the insurance money. They would find out about me for nothing.

Well, shit.

I stared into space for a while, listening to the faint breeze through the trees, looking up into the blue-hot sky. Okay. Nothing more I can do here.

I stood up, hoisting my pack onto my sweaty back. I turned and began walking back the way I had come, trudging slowly, not thinking. I was too tired to think.

Some unknown time later, I arrived at my truck. I dropped my pack, my vest, and my belt, piling them in the back. Once more on the road, I began to think again.

When does self-loathing turn into self-pity? Had I finally crossed that invisible line? How could I tell?

As I drove, it came to me. Yes, self-loathing can bleed over into self-pity, and I was making it so.

If I just mired myself there, living the pain every day, never trying to make a change, then it was self-pity for sure. It would go on forever. The story would be the same, always, because I would never have summoned the courage to change it.

It'd been years since I tried to learn more about transsexualism. There were others like me, I knew. I'd heard the stories, there were new books. Was I just gay? I didn't know. There was so much I didn't know.

As I drove down the road, I thought about what had just happened. What stopped me? It was pure fear, I realized. Fear of dying, fear of discovery. The angry voice in my head was fear talking. It was always fear.

I couldn't continue living like that. Fear was eating me up. The loneliness, too. Somehow, it had to stop. Somehow, I had to quit hiding from myself and find out what I was.

185

TRANS-FORMATIONS

Twenty-Seven

New Research - 1990

I couldn't believe my eyes. There, on the library shelf, was an entire section of books on transgenderism! Oh my god, where do I start?!

Okay, cool your jets, I thought. You're not a psychologist, so some of the jargon in the professional books will be unintelligible. Best to start with the popular stuff, perhaps a memoir. There was one, *Conundrum,* written by Jan Morris. As a male he was a mountain climber and explorer, an adventure travel writer, and was even in the British military, but transitioned later in life. It sounded much like my story. There was also one about the tennis player who transitioned, Renee' Richards. She called hers *Second Serve.*

I started with those two, to see if their stories rang true for me, and began to read.

Months later, the company issued me a laptop computer to take into the field. File your reports this way, they said. Sure thing, I replied.

Of course, the first thing I searched for on the new "World Wide Web" was information about transsexualism....

So that's what I am, I thought as I stared at the screen.

There was a name for what I felt; "gender identity disorder." As many as a million people in the United States suffered from it. It seemed to result from many factors: hormonal chemistry in the womb resulting in a feminine brain structure seemed to be the present thinking. It was also important to understand the difference between sexual attraction and gender identity, it said. The way I had lived, hiding in my "granite shell," pretending to be a "real man," all that bullshit? Others had done the same.

It told me that I was not a "fetishistic narcissist" as that textbook had labeled me so long ago.

My entire life, I'd felt like the only person in the world fighting this demon. I'd been able to push it down for long stretches of time, but it always found a way to claw back to the surface at unexpected times, getting new air for the next battle. It was called a "binge-purge" cycle.

I am transgender. I am not the only one.

Reading on, I looked for a path.

Okay, so, now what? I thought. My choices don't look too good. If I "come out," there's a high risk of losing Barb, losing my job, and alienating her family and what would be left of mine, plus all our friends. I'll end up unemployed because no one will hire me. Barb will leave me, and I'll have nowhere to go. If I'm lucky perhaps I'll be able to wander the streets with a grocery cart full of clothes. Women's clothes.

And what would Barb do? She couldn't afford the house on her salary alone. She'd have to sell it and move home with her parents. She'd have alimony from me after the divorce, but if I were unemployed there wouldn't be a salary to pay it.

Worse, I agonized, by staying in the closet all these years, I had taken the best years of her life. We were supposed to grow old together. Instead she'd be a middle-aged woman alone with nowhere to go and a duplicitous ex-husband to blame for it. Could she re-marry? Perhaps, but the odds wouldn't be good. How could I do that to her?

And Mom, my sisters, our friends? What of them? I've deceived them too. Would my coming out affect them? Would people shun them because of me?

Is it just selfish to consider coming out? Is it selfish to want to live? I stared at the screen, considering my options. Ultimately, there were only two.

One, I could remain in my shell and continue doing what I'd been doing, living in fear, living a lie every single day. But that road had brought me to the brink of suicide already. I knew it would again. Two, if I wanted to stay alive, it was simple—I must take the only path that offered a chance of living.

The other path was a dead end—literally.

That night, I dreamed I was standing inside a teepee. I don't know why, but I must get out. I cannot walk. It seems I cannot move in any direction but up.

I look down at my pale, naked body. It is young, strong, and female. There are breasts, softly firm, budding from my chest. The legs are narrow and shapely, the feet slim and tapered. I feel the lightness of this body, the strength of it. Yes, I say to myself. Yes.

I lift my arms above my head and tilt my head back. I feel my hair for the first time as it brushes my shoulders. I can't see it, but I know it is blonde. Shifting my hips to the left, I stand on tip-toe. Gently, I rise off the ground. Just a few inches, but it is enough. I glide through the entryway of the teepee, and the sky above opens to me.

"Come," it says. "Come glide my currents, my streams. They are yours."

I shift to the right, then the left, and rise again. Ten feet now, and the feeling of altitude is gaining strength. Another shift and I begin to find the rhythm of it. It is an inner music I ride, gliding, shifting gracefully from side to side, arms moving as if directing a sweet symphony made of air.

Higher now, I look to the earth below. As I sweep overhead, forests and fields pass by, then a park here, a building there. The wind is a sweet current carrying me along.

As I glide, the buildings begin to pack together. They seem taller, dirtier. I spy something else, wires. There are wires strung across the streets like the grid of a jail, a cage. I cannot land there.

But I don't care. I will stay here, I say. I am safe, swimming the air, my body lithe and responsive. I am free.

Soaring now, higher and higher, five thousand, ten thousand feet, I am a streak of sinuous lightning, bolting upwards to the stratosphere. I see the curve of the earth, the purple horizon in the distance.

But I am too high now. I have gone too far.

I slow, moving less, and begin to lose altitude. My arms spread wide, I feel the air pass through my fingers, across my breasts. My hair comes into view in wispy waves. It is somehow a dark color now, dull brown, ragged and dry.

I plummet toward the earth below. It takes on form, then detail. The wires are everywhere. They are a trap. There will be no flying here, they say. Not for you.

I twist, I turn, I flap my arms in desperation. Nothing. I fall, a helpless bird, slamming into a web of steel and dirt and hate, ripping my body, shredding me into nothingness.

I wake up. My pillow is wet with tears.

TRANS-FORMATIONS

Twenty-Eight

Oh, Mom - 1990

Four of us, dirty and sweaty from a long hot day in the Oregon desert, trudged into the lobby of our hotel in Ontario, Oregon. We were reconnaissance sampling for gold and other metals at some of the old prospect sites in the Oregon desert, but hadn't seen anything exciting. We all looked forward to a hot shower, a cold beer, and a meal, in that order.

"Is one of you Rick Shepard?" the desk clerk asked as we approached the desk. She seemed disturbed.

"Yes, I'm Rick Shepard." I thought perhaps there was a problem with the bill. Or perhaps they had discovered my green case filled with women's clothes.

"We received an emergency call for you from your office this afternoon. Here's the number; you should call right away."

I turned to my fellow geologists. "Guys, I'll meet you in the bar as soon as I can."

"Take your time, Rick. We'll wait to hear from you."

I quickly headed down the long hallway from the lobby to my room. The number the front desk gave me was my home number. Has something happened to Barb? I worried.

The phone rang once.

"Hello?" It was Barb's voice.

"Barb, it's me! What's wrong? Are you okay? I just got back from the field and got the message to call."

"I'm fine, honey. It's not me, it's your Mom. She's had a stroke. It looks like she may have had it on Saturday, and lay on the floor of her house for at least a day and a half, maybe more. The neighbors found her this morning. The fire department had to break down the door."

"Do you know how she's doing?"

"No, but I called Brenda. She's on her way there now."

"Thank you, sweetie. I'll get the next plane out."

Less than twenty-four hours later, I walked into the hospital in Kansas City, tired and worried. I turned and walked down the long, sterile hallway, smelling of isopropyl alcohol and floor wax, checking the numbers on the walls beside the shiny wood doors.

There it is: Shepard, 451.

The door was partially open. I stopped, knocked, then stepped inside.

Both Brenda and Barbara were in the room. Brenda was sitting in the window seat looking uncomfortable and worried, while Barbara sat in a chair next to Mom's bed.

Brenda had married just a few months before Barb and me, and had two children of her own. She lived in a small town on the Oregon coast. Barbara had married, but her husband had developed leukemia and passed away. She still lived in Kansas City, and was raising her young daughter, with Mom's help.

194

Mom was lying in her hospital bed, awake. Her hair was a thick, lush white, cut in a page-boy. It startled me for a moment, reminding me of the picture of her as a child I had seen so many years ago in the bottom of that tall secretary at home.

When she heard me walk in, she turned. Her eyes widened when she saw me. She stretched out her right arm, a crooked look of joy on her face.

"Awwl! Ickad! Ickad!" she squawked.

I moved to her hospital bed and bent down to her. We hugged, awkwardly, for a long moment.

I was stunned. This is awful, I thought. Oh my god, no, this can't be!

When she let go, I stepped around the bed to Brenda, then Barbara, giving each a quick hug in turn.

"Have you talked with the doctor?" I asked.

"Yes, he was here this morning. He said the stroke is severe because she went so long before she was found. She's paralyzed on her left side, and can't talk. She understands okay, I think, but seems confused. That's all we know. He hasn't been back to see us, or tell us anything. He's kinda arrogant. He's head of the department or something."

"Barbara, when did you get here?"

"I came this morning. The doctor had already come and gone by that time."

"Anything since then?"

"No, the nurses come in every once in a while and check her blood pressure and pulse. That's about it. The IV she's got in her arm is to keep her hydrated, they said. She can't swallow real good right now."

"Shit," I said.

"Yeah," Barbara replied. "Totally."

"I'll ask at the nurse's station when we might see that doctor again. Anyway, I suspect it's been a long day for you guys. Do you wanna go home? Brenda, do you have a car to get around?"

"I'm using Mom's car while I'm here, so no problem, and I've made the extra bed so you can stay at Mom's house too. We can coordinate stuff from there. Yeah, I'm tired. Are you gonna stay for a while?"

"Yes, I'll stay, then I'll be back early to see if I can catch that doctor. Okay?" I asked, looking at Barbara.

"Yeah, that'll be fine." she replied. "I'll be back tomorrow afternoon." She seemed distant.

They hugged Mom, then we hugged each other at the hospital room door. As they walked down the hall to the elevator, I turned back to the room.

Mom was looking at me, her good arm raised up to me to pull me close. I walked over to her bed and leaned down, putting my arms around her.

The hospital smell was there, mixed with the smell of my Mother: the pilot, the hard working government employee, the daughter of an oppressive old tyrant, the woman who raised three kids in the 1950s and 60s largely by herself.

"I love you, Mom," I whispered as we hugged.

It was then she began to cry—deep, ragged sobs, full of despair. We cried together, she and I, for an eternity.

❧

We assembled in Mom's hospital room again four days later. We had talked amongst ourselves, and decisions had been made. The hospital was going to discharge her, we were told, after just two weeks of minimal rehabilitation. Then they'd ship her to some local nursing home and be done with it. It had become clear to all of us over the last few days that she could never go home again, especially after so little care. But we sure as hell were not going to stick her in a nursing home to die.

Neither of my sisters was in a position to take care of Mom. Both Brenda and Barbara had children to raise. It was up to me as the oldest, as the solvent one, as the "man of the house," to do something.

"Mom, here's what we think will work best, but if you don't like it we will try to figure out something else. We all think two weeks of rehab is not enough, but that's all this hospital has to offer. That's what your doctor is recommending. He's an arrogant jackass, by the way, and we're not accepting that."

Mom began nodding vigorously when I said "jackass," and surprising all of us, said "Yes!" in a clear, firm voice. Clearly, she understood. We had been told that she might be able to say certain words or phrases she habitually used before the stroke. We looked at each other, smiling.

There was hope in that little word.

"So here's the deal. We'd like to move you to Denver to be near me and my Barb. There's an excellent rehab hospital there, and we've arranged for a six-week program to get you functioning as well as possible. Depending upon how you do, we'll then get you into a good assisted-living center close to us. We can't move you into our house, 'cause it's a split-level, and both Barb and I work. A lot will fall on her, because I'm gone so much, but it's the best we can think of right now. Do you think that sounds okay?"

Mom looked at me, then nodded her head. I sensed she wanted to say something, to ask a question, anything, but the words weren't there. I thought I knew what she wanted to know.

"Mom, this will be expensive. Your health insurance and Medicare will cover some of it, at least the medical part, but to make it work we've got to sell your house. I'm sorry, but we can't see any way around it. The assisted-living apartment will be expensive, but if we've got money from the house stashed away, we think we can swing it."

She looked down at her lap for a long moment, then back up at me. Slowly, she nodded, tears in her eyes. She had worked so hard to get her own house, to get away from Grampa. She had only been in it a few years. Brenda and Barbara went to her, hugging her, comforting her. I just looked at my feet, the good son bringing bad news. I hesitated, steeling myself for the next step, the one that would make it all too real, the one that would profoundly affect the paths of our lives going forward.

"All right Mom, there's one more thing. So we can start to get things moving, we need to have you sign a Power of Attorney. I called your lawyer, and he drafted one for us. I've got it with me. A couple of the nurses can be witnesses, and they have a notary in the hospital we can call. We can sign it today, if you're up to it."

We moved Mom to Denver where Barb and I arranged a six-week stay at a well-respected rehabilitation hospital. We sold her car and, eventually, sold her house. Her old life was gone. She now faced the challenge of creating a new one.

She did not give up. She worked at her rehabilitation, straining to regain skills she needed to live in an assisted-living apartment rather than a full-care nursing home.

She succeeded, despite the devastating effects of the stroke. She could no longer speak in sentences. The left side of her body was paralyzed and she was in a wheelchair. Nevertheless, she wheeled her way from place to place on her own, lived in her own apartment, and made her wishes clear with the words she had plus pantomime.

As best we could, Barb and I became her caregivers, and as we came to understand her in this new language, we settled into a routine, thankful that her dogged determination had made all our lives, including hers, a little easier than they might have been.

TRANS-FORMATIONS

Twenty-Nine

Mom Flies Again - 1993

Three years later, yet another change came into our lives. The Denver office of my company was shut down. I was offered a position at the headquarters office in Reno.

Barb had left the University a few years earlier and found work with the Environmental Protection Agency as a legal clerk, a job she enjoyed. Mom had settled in to her assisted-living apartment and had many friends among the residents. The crux of our decision to go, however, was financial. Barb did not earn enough money to support us on her own. The job market for geologists in Denver was not good, so I would probably face long-term unemployment if we stayed.

"Hey, sweetie, I've got an idea for a present for Mom on Christmas."

We had been in Reno for a year and a half. Mom had settled into her new assisted-living facility, and Barb had found work as an assistant to the president of a non-profit charity. The job was not as satisfying as the one in Denver, but it helped pay the bills. I

was posted as the Project Geologist on an advanced gold exploration program in eastern Nevada, working ten days out, four days
home.

"What'd you have in mind?"

"Let's arrange for a flight in a small plane over Reno to see
the lights. It's something she did for us kids back when we lived
in Kansas City."

"Hey, she'll love it. Let's do it!"

The next day I visited Sierra Flying Service at the Reno airport. They were willing despite Mom's handicap, especially when
I told them that she had been a flight instructor herself. I took Mom
out for lunch on Sunday as usual, and told her of the plan.

"So, Mom, do you want to give it a shot?" I asked her over her
favorite lunch of a massive chicken burrito drenched in hot salsa.

"Yes!" was the clear and emphatic reply, delivered with broad
smile.

The following weekend was clear and crisp: perfect flying
weather. We took Mom to dinner, then at dusk drove to the airport
where the pilot was waiting for us. He had found a solid wooden
box of about the right height, so we rolled Mom in her wheelchair
onto the tarmac and over to the plane.

"Ooh!" Mom said as we got closer.

It was a pretty white Cessna with a wide blue stripe down the
side, gleaming in the airport lights. We rolled under the left wing
and positioned the box next to the aircraft. Mom's strong side was
her right, so we thought she would have a better time of it climbing
in from there.

We tried everything, but she couldn't keep her balance when
bending over under the wing. Mom, however, was not to be de-

terred. She was going on this flight no matter what, so she solved the problem for us: she stepped up onto the box, pivoted and sat on the floor in the back of the plane. The pilot and I were then able to scoot her backwards and awkwardly lift her into the back seat. I sat in the back with her, while Barb took the co-pilot's seat. We were ready.

We lifted off into the smooth night sky of Reno. I watched Mom as she scrutinized the pilot, the gauges, the world outside, grinning with joy. Gaining altitude, we banked to the east and then turned north, circling the city in a counter-clockwise direction a thousand feet above the ground.

The casinos stood out like brightly-lit birthday cakes, tall and garish, their blazing lights creating a dancing glow on the underside of our wings. The poor little Christmas lights, scattered here and there, had no chance.

After a few minutes circling the city, we flew northward, passing the city limits to cruise over the desert, a half-moon and clear star-sprinkled sky lending a soft, eerie glow to the land. Below us in a valley, a single road cut through the landscape, the headlights of trucks and cars creeping along like a trail of incandescent insects bound for the horizon. The mountains on either side cut massive black silhouettes out of the sky, their ridge lines and peaks silver-sharp in the moonlight.

An hour later we landed and wheeled into the flight service office to do the paperwork and pay the bill. Mom rolled into the small waiting area. She pivoted and began pointing at me.

"Ooh, ooh, ooh," she said emphatically, pointing at me with her finger. "Ooh, ooh, ooh."

"Are you okay, Mom? Do you need to go to the bathroom?"

"Ooh,ooh,ooh," she said, shaking her head no and pointing at me. "Ooh!"

It dawned on me what she wanted. She wanted me to learn to fly. She wanted to give me a chance to experience what she herself loved, what had been such a big part of her life: flying.

"You want me to learn to fly?"

"Yes!"

"Mom, are you sure about that? It's expensive."

"Poo!"

We had never heard her say that word, but I was pretty sure I understood what she meant.

"Okay Mom. I'd like to learn. If you're sure . . . ."

"Yes!"

"Barb?" I asked, turning to her.

"Of course!" she said, smiling. She knew I had always wanted to fly.

I started classes, and six months later I received my pilot's license.

Thanks to Mom, I had fulfilled a part of that secret dream I had when I was a kid—to be just like her.

Two years later, our lives took yet another turn. The company offered me the chance to be part of a new office in Vancouver, British Columbia. Once again, my career and my income determined the outcome.

It wasn't all bad, however. Since our time in Oregon, Barb and I had long wanted to return to the Pacific Northwest. This was our chance. Mom just shrugged and nodded. She understood the way of things.

Thirty

It Rains Here - 1996

"So, this lovely three-bedroom ranch has just under two thousand square feet, plus a huge two-car garage with a half-bath and 450-square-foot shop. It sits on four and a half acres, and has a view of Mt. Baker, if you look through those trees over there. It's already fenced as you can see, and it's zoned for agricultural use, including pasture for horses or cows. Lots of dairies around here, as you may have noticed. Also lots of berry fields."

As the real estate agent droned on, Barb and I looked around. It was a fairly new place with beige vinyl siding and what they called a "hipped" roof, sitting in open, flat country amid similar properties. It was nothing to get excited about architecturally, but whatever Barb wanted was fine by me.

Barb had given up a lot those last years, as we moved to follow my career. More, her mother had recently died of cancer. Barb had made several trips to her parents' home in Washington State to care for her in her last months, a grueling and emotional experience. It was long past time for Barb to enjoy the fruits of her labors.

After the tour inside, we were standing in the driveway. Barb and I looked at each other and Barb gave the merest nod. She wanted it. We had talked about getting horses, and this would be her chance. In a way, it would be her dream home.

"Can you tell me how far it is to downtown Vancouver?" I asked, turning to the agent. "I'll be doing the commute every day."

"I think it's about sixty miles," she replied, "But you can get one of those express passes to go through the border. That makes it a whole lot easier and faster."

We discussed a few other details of the property. I looked again at Barb, then turned to the agent and said "We'd like to put in an offer, I think. Okay, Barb?"

"Yes, I like it too. Let's make an offer."

"Oh, that's marvelous!" the agent gushed. She was going to make a lot of money on the transaction.

We moved August 1st. I drove to the Customs and Border Patrol office and applied for a pass, while Barb looked for work in Bellingham, a town of about 60,000 people. She found a job as a paralegal secretary in the county prosecutor's office, and also signed up for on-line courses to finish a degree in paralegal studies. I commuted an hour and a half each way to work in Vancouver and occasionally went to the field to review property submittals, but rarely for more than a week.

My green Aer Lingus bag, now bulging with my acquisitions, was carefully hidden in the garage among the tools and boxes of books. I used it whenever I could.

A few months later, winter arrived in the Pacific Northwest. That meant low gray skies with drizzle, followed by light rain, followed by fog with drizzle, then perhaps wind with intermittent rain.

No wonder they drink coffee by the gallon up here, I mused.

My office, on the twelfth floor of a downtown Vancouver building, creaked a little in the early evening quiet. The streets below were lit by yellowish lights and lines of cars bumper-to -bumper, headlights glaring, each trying to escape the wet, busy streets to flee into the suburbs at the end of the day. I barely heard them save for the occasional angry honk or grind of a bus.

I sat at my desk looking out over my computer at the scene below. My report was done, the front door was locked. There was no one else in the office. It was time.

My hands shaking just a bit, I pulled up the Yahoo Search page and typed "transgender" into the search line. I hit Enter.

"CHICKS WITH DICKS! Log on NOW! Beautiful and...."

"TRANSSEXUALS ON LINE! Call IMMEDIATELY to meet."

"SHE-MALES READY! HOT and waiting for YOUR call."

"SUSANS PLACE - News and support for the Transgender."

"KINKY TRANNIES! Log on for the thrill of a lifetime."

"Damn!" I said out loud. "That's not what I want!"

But one web site in the list looked serious. Susan's Place. News and support, it said. Clicking on the link, I went to the About Us page.

Susan's Place called itself a peer support group. There were many links leading to a range of information, including hormone therapy, surgery, and the legal ramifications of transition. There was a moderated chat room to talk with others, sharing your story.

Talk with others? I almost cried.

There were others, others like me. I could communicate with them. I would not be alone any more. Yet I paused, pondering the impact of what lay ahead. I was crossing a threshold. My life might change forever if I pressed the key. For good or bad, there would be no going back.

But I knew I could no longer just stare in the mirror, ashamed of the image before me. The barrier I had built between the world and myself, my great egg-shaped granite shell, was cracked. A narrow crack, raggedy-edged and dangerous. But light was coming in. Just a little.

I learned a great deal over the ensuing months. Most importantly, I was no longer alone. I talked with the others, all in as much pain if not more. Like me, most had considered suicide. A few had "transitioned," and told their stories in the chat room. I inhaled every word.

I followed links to surgeons' websites, psychological papers, books, other chat rooms, clothing, and a whole world of information and support that I had not known existed. I found a path forward.

But it would not be easy.

PART THREE

Metamorphic

Heat, pressure, and time are the tools of metamorphism. It is at the very edge of continents where such conditions come together. There, the plates of the earth are always moving, grinding against one another, pushing and pulling rocks into the depths. There, the rocks must change. They must adapt to the conditions around them. Yet even as they lose their original shape and structure, their composition remains the same.

At some point in our lives, we may stop to look at where we are. We ask ourselves, is this where I planned to be, so many years ago? Am I happy with this life? For some, the answer is a simple yes, and we continue, changing little. For others, it is a crisis. We must change or die.

TRANS-FORMATIONS

Thirty-One

Slippery Slope - 1997

"The doctor will see you now," said the young receptionist behind the counter. "It's room 338, down the hall on your left."

"Thanks," I nodded.

It felt like a dream. I was sweating. It was cold and rainy outside, and my armpits were wet, my palms slick, my heart in my throat.

I walked slowly down a long corridor, broken at regular intervals by identical doors. It was an average office suite building, the kind that independent professionals and consultants tended to inhabit—architects, engineers, psychologists and the like. The black and white plastic tags on the doors said "Dr. So-And-So," or "So-And-So, P. Eng.," or "So-And-So, Ph.D."

I scanned each door as I walked, looking for the door labeled "Dr. Sandra Krympe, Ph.D." Doctor Sandra, according to the Yellow Pages, was a psychologist specializing in "sexual disorders."

There it is.

I paused, wiping my hands on my pants, then knocked. The door opened a few seconds later.

213

"Hello, you must be Richard," she said as she extended her hand. "Please come in."

Dr. Sandra appeared to be in her late forties, slim with shoulder-length blonde hair. She was well-dressed, wearing a mid-calf length plaid wool skirt and tall leather boots in a kind of "horse-woman" style, complete with complementary sweater and scarf. We shook hands, then she indicated I sit on the couch by the window. Picking up a notebook from her desk, she sat down on another couch facing me. We engaged in small talk for a minute, then she settled in and asked, "Well, Richard, to start with, why don't you tell me a little bit about yourself."

I took a long, deep breath, then began.

"Okay," I said, voice unsteady. "Well, umm, I'm a minerals exploration geologist. I got my Master's Degree at Oregon State in '79. My job is to explore for metal deposits in hopes of finding one that can be turned into a mine. It's taken me to ten countries over the last twenty years or so, usually working out in the hinterlands. You know, "helicopter in the wilderness" type stuff. I've been married for twenty-seven years now—no kids. I'm gone too much and my wife, Barbara, is career-oriented. We long ago agreed, no children."

"So, are you happy in your relationship with Barbara?"

"I love her very much, but we've had some rough times. We could probably work on our communication."

"Does she love you?"

"Yes, I think so."

"What about your childhood? Was it happy?"

"Not really."

"Can you tell me a bit about it? It would give me a better picture."

"Well, I grew up in Kansas City, Missouri in the fifties and sixties in what was then called a broken home. I've got two younger sisters. Our Mom raised us as best she could, but that required going to her father for help. Grampa owned our car and house, and thought that meant he owned us too. He was a staunch member of the John Birch Society, to give you an idea of what he was like."

"He's passed away?"

"Yes, in 1975."

"And did you ever see your father again after the divorce?"

"No."

"How old were you when that happened?"

"I was seven."

"And your mother and sisters? Where are they now?"

"My mother had a major stroke in 1990. That's when Barb and I became her caregivers. She lives in an assisted-living apartment here in Bellingham. My middle sister is married and lives in Oregon, and the youngest still lives in Kansas City."

She nodded. "Anything else?"

"Mom remarried when I was fifteen. The guy was nice at first, but turned into a selfish child once he got in the door. He and I were headed for trouble when my Mom signed me up in the Navy at age seventeen. I became a weatherman on an aircraft carrier in Vietnam in '67 and '68."

"Thank you Richard," she said, putting down her pen and pad and settling back on the sofa. "That helps a lot. So now, what brings you to me?"

There it was. The precipice. The cliff I had faced in Idaho that hot, dusty summer. The absolute lifelong terror of being discovered. I was about to utter the words that would possibly ruin my life—or make it bearable.

Fear was there, too, whispering in my ear. "Are you sure about this," it said? "Are you so selfish that you can throw yourself over this cliff, ruining your life and the lives of those you love? You could stop now. You don't have to do this. You can just keep on. Sure you can. Just walk out, that's all. Just walk out."

Yet I knew it was a lie. One of those drunken nights in a motel room would kill me, one way or another. It was still a simple choice, the same choice I had been avoiding for years.

It was nearly a minute before I could respond.

"I feel like I'm jumping off a cliff here," I said, voice cracking.

"Well, this is a safe place to do it. Take your time."

A long, painful pause, then: "I am a transvestite, or possibly transgender. I have been cross-dressing in secret for most of my life."

She didn't blink. The floor didn't open up and swallow me, although it seemed the planet ceased spinning on its axis for a brief moment. At least I didn't throw up. I could have. I wanted to. It would have been less humiliating than what I had just done.

After a moment she spoke.

"Ah, yes," she said, compassion in her eyes. "I believe I can help you with that."

I spent the remainder of the hour sobbing, answering her gentle questions, speaking as best I could from the bottom of that dark, steep cliff I had just thrown myself over, surrounded by the ragged chunks of my shattered granite shell.

❧

In secret, I continued to meet with Dr. Sandra. At these sessions she gently questioned me about the details of my past, my feelings, and what I hoped for the future. At times it was painful, at times embarrassing, and often terrifying. I held nothing back. I needed to learn about myself, I needed to learn if I was, indeed, a "fetishistic narcissist." Her lips pressed tightly together when I told her about that term, signaling her understanding of the profoundly detrimental influence it had had on me.

As we talked I knew that at some point there would be a reckoning. I'd have to make the unavoidable decision: what do I do? Do I risk everything?

And what about the repercussions for Barb, for Mom? It wasn't just me that would be affected. Everyone I knew would have to be told. Like a stone tossed into a puddle, the ever-expanding ripples would affect other lives as well. Barb would have to "come out" to her friends and co-workers. Mom would find that it was no longer her son taking her to lunches on Sundays. My sisters, my friends, my employer, all would have to be told. My coming out would affect everyone I knew to a greater or lesser degree.

Again I wondered—am I just being selfish to even consider this path? Shouldn't I just "buck up" and "be a real man?" After all, I'd been doing it for nearly forty years.

"No," Dr. Sandra said, "You can't. And you know that too, don't you? You wouldn't be here otherwise."

Silence for a long moment, then:

"Yes, I know."

❧

It was a rainy Saturday morning, gray and cold. We had finished our breakfast. Barb was sitting on the sofa near the big picture window, reading a magazine.

She was surprised when I handed her the letter, looking up at me with a quizzical look on her face. I couldn't look her in the eye. I moved to the other side of the room and sat down in one of our recliners in front of the television. It was not on.

The room was silent as I waited for our marriage to dissolve. I waited to see if she would scream, or cry, or hit me. I waited to see if she would run to the kitchen for a knife to stab me over and over. I wouldn't blame her, I wouldn't defend myself. I deserved it.

In the reflection of the dead television screen I watched as she flipped back and forth through the pages, re-reading portions here and there.

March 1, 1997

Dear Barb:

This is a very difficult letter for me to write, but it seemed the best way to set down in a somewhat orderly fashion the things I need to tell you.

I'm seeing a psychologist for depression. It has come about due to a long period of stress that apparently depressed the levels of serotonin in my body, among other effects. This is what the psychologist, Dr. Sandra Krympe, told me on my first visit to her when I described my lack of motivation, difficulty concentrating on my work, and the bouts of tears for no immediate reason. But that is not the primary reason I went to see her. In fact, her diagnosis came as a surprise to me.

218

No, the depression is a symptom, a consequence of a particular source of stress I've been living with my entire adult life. I once tried to tell you of this, but I couldn't get the words out. I wish I'd had the courage then, but I didn't. But I must tell you now.

Barb, my love, I am a transvestite, or crossdresser. Specifically, a heterosexual transvestite, although Dr. Krympe has indicated I might be transgender. She has suggested I begin attending a local support group.

Barb, I often have dressed up as a woman when you've been gone from the house for long enough, or when I was in the field in the hotel rooms at night. I've always stayed behind closed doors, so I'm "in the closet" as they say. This is why I went to see Dr. Sandra: to talk, finally, with someone about what I am. I have never told anyone else this in all my life.

Why do I feel it necessary to tell you this now? There are several reasons. First and foremost, I can no longer continue to be untruthful to you, in that this is a "sin of omission" by not telling you. Although I've never said it well, I love you. I've shared every part of me with you except this one. The shame and guilt I have felt for this has hurt me, and I suspect you've sensed over the years that I've not been completely open to you in our marriage. I've cried myself to sleep many times for the shame of it. For a long time I told myself that if I were discovered I would kill myself, the guilt was so profound. Several times over the years I came close to killing myself in an "accident" so as to be sure you got the insurance and could move on with your life without me. But I eventually realized that I did not want to die.

I cannot say this enough: I am still me and I love you. My feelings for you have never wavered. This is absolutely not "your fault," but is something that has been with me since puberty, and probably before that. When we married I thought this need in me would go away. It did for a long while, but returned. I have since learned that it never goes away, that it is not curable by shrinks or doctors, that the only treatment is acceptance.

Another reason I tell you now is the loneliness. It's hard to describe, but a part of me lives in a box (that closet). I have yearned to talk with someone, with you, without fear of being regarded as a repulsive, perverted thing. But fear and guilt are difficult emotions to overcome. I am hoping that by coming out to you now, our communication will become better and more open in the future.

Barb, I love you and want you to love me. All of me, without condition or reservation. In our own unique way we have a strong marriage. I honestly think that with this out in the open our communication can improve. The fact that it hasn't always been so is clearly my fault. Please, let's try. I want to help you understand this side of me. I also want to alleviate as much as possible any strain, confusion, and pain this might cause you. I will always be here for you, if you want me.

Rich

The room remained silent as she read. Air did not move, dogs did not bark, water did not run downhill, grass did not grow. Even the light outside the window was the featureless gray light of a featureless gray day, indifferent, unchanging, hard as steel. Barb didn't cry or make any noise, she didn't shift her weight or move. She just read it, over and over.

I waited.

Finally she finished. She stood up, the letter clutched in her hand. She walked over to me and put her right hand on my shoulder.

"It's okay. I just don't want to see it."

She went to the bedroom and closed the door. I sat for a few minutes, dazed, not knowing what came next, not able to think, tears leaking out of my eyes. Eventually I stood up and walked to the back room, sitting down in front of the computer. I stared at the dark screen for a long time, doing nothing.

TRANS-FORMATIONS

Thirty-Two

Opening the Door - 1997

"Yes sir, that's a thirty by thirty sheet-metal-clad pole barn with two horse stalls. When could you come by to see the site and talk about it? Okay, that'd be fine. Thanks, see you then." I hung up the phone.

"Barb, they'll be over on Saturday morning to give us a quote. That okay?"

"Yeah, that'll be fine. I don't meet with Julie until noon."

Julie was Barb's friend from college in Denver, who now lived in the Seattle area. She had started making trips to see Barb within a week or two of my letter. Julie never talked to me about it, but I didn't mind. She was here for Barb.

We fell back into our usual patterns of conversation, except that I now slept in the spare bedroom, and the phrase "I love you" was not uttered any more. There was a terrible tension underlying our interactions. When I tried to talk to Barb, to open a discussion, she replied, "There's nothing to talk about," her voice tight with anger. I didn't press her.

At least the dogs still loved me.

As I had promised, we were requesting bids to build a small barn for two horses she had picked out, Twister and Gracie. Twister was a big gray Appaloosa mare, Gracie a sweet-tempered little roan mare. We also drew up plans for a large box garden. We planned a dozen knee-high boxes to be built in a geometric pattern with an integral sprinkler system so we could grow flowers and vegetables.

We embraced the country life like a lifeboat at sea.

Meanwhile, I began attending weekly meetings with a local transgender support group. Tuesday nights I went out to the small utility bathroom in the garage where I got dressed. I put on my clothes, adding just a little light makeup and a bit of jewelry. Up top, however, I wore a sports jacket or man's shirt, and had slacks and shoes in the back seat, just in case. I left the house that way, waiting until I had driven some distance. Often, I parked in a stand of trees along the road into town, sometimes behind the big dumpster of a store. There, I finished dressing in the car. I didn't want Barb to see me, per her request, let alone the neighbors.

Each time I drove to a meeting I was petrified at the thought of being stopped by the police and arrested. I was sure it would make the local paper. I could just imagine the headlines:

Transvestite Arrested in Bellingham
Caught Checking His Makeup in Rear View Mirror

Then my employer would find out and I'd be fired. We'd lose the house because I could no longer find work, then we'd lose our marriage, if it wasn't lost already. I'd become the newest homeless person before I could say "shopping cart." It would all happen after I had been repeatedly raped in jail, of course.

Once a week I put everything I valued in my life at risk. It was terrifying.

"So, to qualify for gender reassignment surgery from a reputable surgeon you must abide by the Harry Benjamin Standards of Care. Harry Benjamin was a New York psychiatrist who published a book in 1966 that is still the definitive text on the subject and recommendations for treatment. The foundation established in his name currently recommends that patients have at least two psychological professionals, one with a Ph.D., diagnose them with "Gender Identity Disorder." Then you must live a full year in your preferred gender before your surgical date. That includes making a living, being out, and all that. It's called the Real Life Test. You can't just be a weekend warrior."

A nervous murmur went through our small group of ten. The speaker was a psychologist from Seattle. She had been willing to come up to Bellingham to speak with us. She had recently expanded her practice to include transsexuals, and was looking for patients.

"One last hurdle—the surgeon can say no, but that usually occurs only if he or she decides you're not a good risk to survive the surgery. If you're in decent physical condition, it's not a problem."

One of the others raised her hand. "Why all these requirements? They seem so arbitrary. Just a way to make us jump through hoops and pay more money."

"Yes, I'm sure it feels that way. But this is a one-way trip, and everyone involved wants to be absolutely sure that it's right for you, that you can make the transition psychologically and physically, and that you can survive afterward. The guidelines aren't written in stone, though. The Harry Benjamin organization reviews the requirements every year to decide if changes need to be made. They may change in the future."

Having a professional at our meetings was rare. Most of the time the meetings were a way to get together and update each other on our progress via a round-the-room "check-in." It gave us a chance to share our burdens and be human again. It helped to talk about the fear of being "outed," of the risks and the silent pain and loneliness of being in the closet. With our jobs, our families and our very existence on the line, it was a way to feel connected.

"Are there any other questions?"

No one had any. We were all contemplating the implications of what she had just told us. It was a lot to process.

"Then I want to thank you for inviting me," she went on. "I make no secret of the fact that I am widening my practice to include the transsexual community with regard to both male-to-female and female-to-male issues. So please, take a card," she invited, smiling.

I took one.

"I'll have a glass of the chardonnay, please."

"Yes, ma'am."

The young waiter was a nice-looking college student and our regular waiter on Tuesday nights after the meetings. He always treated us with respect, calling us "ma'am" or "miss." For that small courtesy, he knew we would tip well.

The place was called Poppe's, a local bistro with seating both inside and outside on an open patio. Tonight we were outside enjoying a cool July evening in the Pacific Northwest—clear skies with just a sliver of moon.

I was wearing one of my new catalog acquisitions, a lovely white shirtdress with large pastel flowers adorning the skirt, and a pair of light blue flower cut-out sandals. Both fit me well, and complemented the honey-blonde of my page-boy style wig. I had done my nails in a subtle pink mauve color—"Desirable" it was called—that went well with my skin tone.

My glass of chardonnay arrived. It was yellow-gold and cool, the glass surface beaded with tiny droplets of condensation. I sat quietly, sipping the wine and enjoying the conversation.

This is what it's supposed to be, I thought. No fear, no angst, just being me. I gazed up at the gauzy moon, just visible in the glare of city lights around us. I looked around the restaurant at the other patrons. No one cared about us. We were just some chatty women on a night out.

For a long moment I looked down at my glass on the table beside me. On the rim was a faint mark of lipstick—my lipstick.

It hit me that this was a replay of that fateful moment so many years ago in Karen's basement when we played dress-up, when we made up stories of ourselves as women with real lives and real feelings. I'm there again, but I'm also here. I'm here: and this time it is real.

God help me—I am Erika.

"So, shall we go to Poppe's again? I'll drive if you like."

Everyone agreed, and we filed out of the meeting room and down the stairs to the street. Poppe's had become a special place to us.

"My car's just around the corner."

Tuesday evenings in downtown Bellingham were quiet, and this night was no exception. There were just enough people around to let us practice not "getting clocked," that is, being identified as cross-dressers, but not enough to intimidate us into hiding ourselves. We were all learning, building our courage day by day.

As we approached the car, I pulled the keys out of my purse and pressed the button to open the doors. Nothing happened. I pressed again, and again no response. By the time we got to the car I realized that the little battery in the key fob must be dead. Damn!

"Girls, I'm sorry, but the door opener seems to be dead."

"Well, now what do we do?" was the reply.

"Well, I can still open the door with the regular key. Thing is, that sets off the alarm. The car honks and the lights flash. We will find ourselves the center of attention, and someone might call the cops."

"Oh no, we don't want that. Any other ideas?"

"Yeah, there might be a way. I don't know if the back doors or the trunk are hooked into the alarm. We could take a chance with the trunk, 'cause the back seat has a center console door. If we get a wire hanger, I could crawl into the trunk, push open that little door and snag a back door latch to open it. If we're lucky it won't set off the alarm."

"Well, okay, if that's the only way."

A few minutes later we were ready.

"Okay, stand around the back of the car like you're just talking. I'll open the trunk with the key."

They gathered around the car, while I inserted the key.

The trunk opened with its usual "clunk," but no alarm. All right! Next step.

Looking around furtively, I pulled up my skirt, a nice brown denim number that flared just a bit, giving the illusion of a waistline, and crawled into the trunk, squirming my way forward to push on the console door. It opened easily. Almost there.

One of the girls handed me the wire hanger, already straightened out but leaving a hook on one end. I put it through the opening, extending my arm into the back seat. I put my head down against the opening, and found that I could just see the rear door latch with one eye. Wiggling and stretching, I got the loop around the latch.

"Okay, here goes."

It was surprising how loud the horn was. As I lay in the trunk, skirt bunched up around my thighs, a gaggle of cross-dressed men at my feet, I suddenly saw our predicament from an observer's perspective. I began to laugh, even as I scrambled to get out of the trunk. I hit my head in my desperation to climb out, pulling my wig down over one eye. I emerged, red-faced, laughing to tears, into the blare of the horn and the flash of lights.

I ran around to the drivers' side door. I opened it with the key, and inserted it into the ignition. The honking and flashing immediately stopped.

In the sudden silence, I looked up from the seat. "Girls," I said, "I think the first round is on me tonight."

TRANS-FORMATIONS

Thirty-Three

The Bad Year - 1998

"I'm sorry to be the bearer of bad news, Rick," said Chris, my boss, "but the company is shutting down the Vancouver office effective March 1st. You and the others in the office are being laid off."

I sat at the conference table, stunned. Laid off? After almost fourteen years with the company?

"Since our mine in Nevada shut down, the company has had to cut costs. Furthermore, the exploration emphasis is moving to South America and our operation in Chile. They're not looking at acquisitions or joint ventures in North America any more. Management has decided that South America is the place to be."

The office in Chile had been open for some time and had had excellent success. They had found a new gold deposit that looked like it could be good enough for development. I had been offered a position there, but had turned it down. I didn't want to do that to Barb, among other reasons.

"I don't know what to say, Chris."

"I know it's a shock, Rick, but because of your long service with the company, you're getting a good severance package.

231

They'll move you back to Reno if you want, and you'll be getting a year's salary and benefits. Plus they've hired a consulting firm to help you find work again."

"Thanks, Chris."

"Here's the details of the severance." Chris slid a fat folder across the table. "Why don't you take a look at it today and talk to Barb. They'd like to know by the end of the week if you're going back to Reno."

We said no to Reno. Somehow, we decided, we'd make it in Bellingham. I would look for work—any kind of work—here. As an American, getting hired by a Canadian company based in Vancouver would be difficult. I'd be competing with Canadian geologists with similar experience but fewer bureaucratic hurdles to overcome with regard to work visas, salary, benefits and other details.

It took ten long months to find a job. I became a chemicals salesman at the local paper mill.

"So Erika," said Dr. Krympe, "How is it going with your hormone therapy? It's been about six weeks, correct?"

"Yes, Dr. Sandra, and I have never been on a worse roller-coaster in my life! I give myself estrogen injections every two weeks. The next day I am down in the dumps, crying at the slightest thing. The day after that I am angry, mad at the world, mad at stupid things. I think it's the testosterone fighting back. Meanwhile, my legs sweat at night. Just my legs. I don't get it. Is menopause like this? That's what it feels like, but I'm doing it backwards!"

"Ha!" Dr Krympe laughed. "That's a good way to put it. It affects people in different ways, but your experience is pretty much the norm. It's not for the faint of heart, that's for sure."

"I guess that makes me feel better. Sort of."

"Have patience, Erika. The symptoms will be less severe as your body adjusts. It takes at least six months for the permanent effects to start showing themselves, so you have time to decide if you want to move forward."

"Okay."

"But at this point in your journey we should begin discussing your future. You must eventually make a decision. Do you want to go through with transition and all that it entails, or do you want to continue living as you have been? We can approach it incrementally, in small steps, but ultimately you will have to decide one way or another."

"Yes, I understand," I said, staring at the floor.

"I have been in contact with your counselor in Seattle, and she concurs with my diagnosis of gender identity disorder. You check all the boxes. We are both willing to write the necessary letters of endorsement should you choose to go forward with gender reassignment surgery."

"This is terrifying," I whispered after a long moment. "This puts everything at risk: my marriage, my job, connections with my family, such as they are. Everything."

"Yes, I'm sorry to say, it does. With regard to your marriage, I feel it is a co-dependent relationship, and as such it is not likely to survive your transition. I know your Seattle counselor agrees. Bluntly put, you should be making preparations for a divorce. Now."

I just stared at the doctor, mouth set, jaw clamped, my mind spinning.

No! I love her. I love Barb. I can't do this!

Yet if I don't I'll probably kill myself one way or another. I've thought of it so many times, at so many gut-churning moments. Especially that cliff in Idaho. So easy, so easy it would have been. Going that way seems easier to contemplate than this. This is painful beyond measure.

Where the hell is love in all of this?

"So, Barb, that's where I am. Both of my counselors agree that I am transgender. They recommend that I start making preparations for surgery."

We sat at our small table in the breakfast nook late on a Saturday morning. The sun was out, but neither of us noticed or cared. Our worlds had become too small to include the weather. I just stared down at the remains of our breakfast, a bowl of granola for her, a cup of bitter coffee for me. Bowl and cup sat side by side on the table, empty. Just like us. Empty.

After a long pause, Barb said, "I want you to see another psychologist or psychiatrist. One who knows about these things. Can you arrange that?"

"Yes, I think so. My counselor in Seattle has contacts with the University of Washington. Would someone from there be okay?"

"Yes."

"I see her on Thursday. I'll make the request."

"All right." She stood up and walked to the bedroom, shutting the door behind her.

"And that's my background, Dr. Hunter. I've cross-dressed on and off since I was eight. I've managed to stay hidden in the closet all that time, but now I feel like I'm going to explode or do something drastic."

Doctor Hunter was Dean of Psychiatric Medicine at the University of Washington Medical School. He had worked with transgender patients for many years, dating back to the late sixties at the Mayo Clinic.

"Have you ever considered suicide?"

"Yes sir, several times. I've come close once, but I realized I didn't want to die. I just wanted to live as a woman. The feeling is overwhelming, and always has been."

"I understand. Tell me, you didn't come to this meeting dressed as Erika today. Why not?"

"Mostly in deference to my wife, Barb. She doesn't want to see me dressed, and we drove down together. She's in the waiting room."

"Would you have been comfortable coming dressed?"

"I would have done it had I been alone, but being comfortable about it is another issue. As you can see, I don't 'pass,' so I need to be careful in public."

"Are you dressed when you attend your support group in Bellingham?"

"Oh, yes."

"And have you attended meetings with the group here in Seattle?"

"Yes, a few times."

"Have you gone out as Erika on your own?"

"Yes, a number of times."

"Were you comfortable being dressed then?"

"Yes, yes I was. I felt self-conscious, and afraid of getting caught or arrested. But when I don't feel self-conscious or afraid, in those times I feel, well, whole, I guess."

"I see. Thank you for your candor," he said, sitting back in his chair. "I also have information from both of your counselors. I'll review it, and we'll set up another appointment in two weeks. I'll meet with your wife at that time. Does that work for you?"

"Yes sir, we can do that. Thank you for your time."

Two weeks later, we drove back to Seattle for the meeting. Barb was in his office for more than an hour, and when she emerged it was clear she had been crying. A lot. She didn't speak as we walked to the car, and I didn't ask.

Not until we merged into the freeway traffic headed north did she say a word. Then, her voice strained, she said, "He says you're transgender."

"Oh."

That's all I said: no relief, no sense of validation. I could say nothing else. I knew I had to wait. In that moment I had to wait to see what came next, wait to see if we had any kind of relationship going forward. I waited to see if we still had a marriage.

After a while she spoke again, voice cracking. "I want you to move out of the house for a while. I need to think things over. I feel awful. It feels like—like you're killing my husband."

With tears welling in my eyes, I whispered, "Okay."

I moved to an apartment in town a few weeks later. I continued to work at the paper mill, continued to attend support group meetings in Bellingham and Seattle. I continued to take care of things at the house after work and weekends, doing all the chores I had done before. I continued to deposit my paycheck into our joint account.

And I continued to agonize over the irrevocable horror I had set in motion.

TRANS-FORMATIONS

Thirty-Four

The Worst Year - 1999

"Do you want to go to the store today, Mom?"

"Yes!" she said emphatically.

Over the nine years since her stroke, we had learned to communicate. The easy, common words she knew were still available to her, but often the communication required looks and gestures. Her body language, a look in her eyes, a throaty noise were all she needed to let me know how she felt or what she wanted.

It was Sunday, the day in every week when I took Mom out to lunch and shopping if I was in town, usually for snacks and—always—chocolate. Her assisted-living facility served good food, but it tended to be bland. Our lunches were a chance to enjoy food with flavor, the spicier the better, and a glass of wine. Today it was the inevitable chicken burrito drenched in salsa and a chardonnay.

"Okay, will do. The grocery store?"

"Ummf," she said. That meant no.

"The drug store?"

"Yes!"

I understood. The drug store wasn't as crowded, so was easier to maneuver for a person in a wheelchair. They also had a good candy aisle.

"Okay, drug store it is," I said, and off we went.

Almost an hour later, I wheeled Mom through another parking lot as she balanced two bags full of candy and two jigsaw puzzles on her lap. She had a big smile on her face. She had scored big at the drug store today. I loaded the wheelchair into the trunk and stashed the bags, then slid into the driver's seat.

I paused for a moment, took a deep breath, then spoke.

"Mom, I've got something I need to tell you."

"Huh?"

"Do you remember when I was a teenager, in high school? I think you were working for the FAA. We lived next door to Grampa, and I would usually get home before anyone else after school. Do you remember that?"

"Unnh," she said, puzzled.

"Do you remember coming home early one afternoon and catching me trying on your clothes? I was upstairs in your room when you came in the front door. I panicked, and ran down the hallway to my room, but I think you saw me. Do you remember that?"

"Unh," she said quietly. Yes.

I stared at the floor as tears welled up in my eyes.

This was it. I had just opened the door, I knew. No going back. Right now, this minute, my Mother was going to lose her son, the one she was so proud of, the successful, masculine scientist and explorer. Her Richard was about to die here in the car in a lousy fucking parking lot.

"Okay, Mom. That was not the only time I did that. In fact, I have been putting on your clothes, and Brenda's and Barbara's, in secret since I was eight.

"Mom, I am what's called a transsexual, or transgender. I've always wanted to be a girl. I've seen three professional counselors about it, and they all agree that that's what I am."

She was silent, looking down at her feet, hands in her lap. I couldn't see her face, couldn't tell if she was crying.

I looked down at my feet too. It was done. I just had to explain the details, that's all. Simple. Just the basics of how her son would soon cease to exist.

I waited. I had dreaded this day perhaps most of all. I was the only son. She had hopes and dreams for me, even now. And worse, since she was dependent upon me and Barb as caregivers, the repercussions would profoundly affect her life.

I waited.

Slowly, she reached over with her good right hand and picked up her left. She leaned over toward me. I thought she might be trying to slap me, or hit me, any way possible she could show her disgust, her disappointment. She began to slap my right knee. Over and over again she slapped it while saying with perfect clarity, "Thank you! Thank you!"

We drove to her apartment. Once settled, we sat, and I continued, telling her the ragged, difficult details of what was to come.

"So, Mom, that's the process. I plan to start what they call the Real Life Test in 2001, a bit more than a year from now. That phase requires living and holding a job as a woman for a year. Then I'll be eligible for surgery. I've chosen the name 'Erika' because it has "rik" in the middle, and in that way a small part of Rick will survive. My middle name will be Jean, like Barb's."

"Right now I have one day a week I call my Erika Day, usually Saturdays. That's the day I dress and go out in public, usually just to the mall or a walk in a park. It's part of the test. But more importantly, I'm testing myself. Anyway, if you call me to do something for you on a Saturday, it will be Erika that shows up at your door, not Richard. Do you understand that?"

"Unnh," she said a bit tentatively. She's overwhelmed, I realized. That's enough for one day. Enough for a lifetime.

"Okay, Mom, that's enough for one day. I'll see you next week as usual, unless you need me sooner. If you do, just call. Okay?"

"I love you, Mom," I said as I bent down to give her a kiss. She grabbed me with her good arm and held me close for an extra second.

"It'll be okay, Mom."

As I left the apartment I dearly hoped I had not just lied to my Mother.

A week later she called. It was a Friday evening. She wanted me to come over to her apartment to do something.

"Okay, Mom, I'll be there in the morning. You realize it will be Erika at the door?"

"Unnh."

"Okay, I'll be there about ten or so. Is that all right?"

"Yes."

A quiet response, but clear. Yes.

She is ready to see me.

Okay. I'll wear the brown denim skirt and my scrunch boots. I look good in that, plus the cream-colored wool sweater and a simple necklace. The "horsewoman" look. I'll wear earrings and makeup, just a little, to top it off. I want to look conservative. I'm not like a drag queen. I don't want to shock her. Oh, no, I don't want to shock my mother.

I sneaked in the back door of her assisted-living residence, hoping I wouldn't encounter any of her friends or staff. As it was a cloudy morning and perfect sleeping weather, I met no one as I climbed the stairs. I got to her floor and stepped into the hallway, heart pounding, peeking around the corner and down the corridor to be sure the coast was clear. Everyone was asleep, it seemed. I walked to her door, paused, then knocked.

"Mom, it's me. Can I come in?"

"Unnh." It sounded tentative, nervous, but perhaps it was my own terror I heard.

With a deep breath, I turned the knob and stepped inside, closing the door behind me. I turned and said, "Hello, Mom."

Her jaw dropped. She made a small noise—not one of her usual noises— that sounded like she had been hit in the stomach. For a moment I worried that she had forgotten our conversation, if she had thought it was just a bad dream. There was no way to know. I had set the process in motion. I was committed. She had to see me.

"Mom, this is Erika, this is me. Remember, I told you? Would you like to talk about it?" I knew that she needed a minute to adjust to the sight of her son dressed as a woman. She needed at least a minute to examine the creature that had just walked in her door, to wonder at it, to look into its eyes.

I could see what she was thinking: Where is my Richard? Is he gone? This can't be! Is this some phase, or terrible mental illness?

Where is my son?!

But she couldn't say any of it. The stroke had taken that ability from her. I could only try to ease the pain and turmoil in her mind, try to soften the blow, try to let her know I loved her no matter what. I wanted her to understand that it was still me, that I would be here for her, if she wanted me.

I took care of the small task she had called me for, then sat down in a chair opposite her.

"So, Mom, I am still here for you and I love you, but this is the crux of it: it will be just over a year before I go "full time." That is, when I begin my Real Life Test and start living all the time as a woman. In the meantime, I will keep on testing myself. More days out as Erika. More time going to shrinks, all that stuff.

"That means, at some point it will be Erika pushing your wheelchair. It will be Erika taking you to lunch, going to the store, taking you to the doctor, all of that. You should realize that most people don't understand, and a lot of them don't want to. I'm an 'abomination' to them, and I will be a target of their hate. Some of that might spill over onto you. Certainly there would be sly comments behind your back, like from some of the other residents here. You understand?"

She nodded.

"Okay. So Mom, there's a decision you can make. You can stay here in Bellingham with me and Barb as your care givers, or you can move to the Oregon coast to be with Brenda. Brenda and I have talked. I've told her everything, and she says they've got a good assisted-living facility down there and they'd be happy to have you come to live there if you choose. So I'd like you to think about it this week. We can get things rolling and have you there before Christmas, if that's your choice. Can you think about it? Let me know next week?"

She nodded again. "Unnh."

"Is that all you need right now?

"Uh, huh."

"All right. I'll see you next week as usual, okay?"

"Yes." She reached up with her good arm to hug me, then suddenly dropped it.

There would be no hug today. Maybe not ever again.

The next week we went to the steakhouse by the harbor. Mom had the lemon chicken breast, which they cut into small pieces for her, and the chardonnay. I had the chicken and chardonnay as well. We went to the drug store after lunch, then back to the apartment with her haul of chocolate. I took her to the bathroom, and busied myself putting things away and updating her pills while waiting. The usual routine. Finally, I heard her moving around in the bathroom, transferring to her chair, flushing. I knocked, then opened the door.

"All done?"

"Yes."

I stepped in, maneuvering myself behind her to push her into the living room and her recliner. When she had made the transfer, I sat down opposite her.

"Mom, have you thought about what we talked about last week?"

She nodded.

"Have you made a decision?"

She nodded again.

"Okay. So, do you want to move to Oregon to be with Brenda?"

"Yes," she whispered.

Yes. There it was. Yes. My mother chose to move away rather than lose her son before her eyes. She chose to move away before she would face the comments, the risk of embarrassment, the shame. Yes. She said yes.

"Okay, Mom. I'll call Brenda."

I sat in the car outside for a while, my stomach churning, my heart aching. The worst things I had imagined were coming true. I was losing all of my self, piece by piece. I'd moved out of the house, away from Barb and our marriage. My mother had decided to move away because of me. I'd even lost my career in geology. I was reduced to a shell, a walking, talking creature with no reason for being.

Two weeks later, Brenda and her husband came up from Oregon with a rental truck. We loaded Mom's things. We hugged and said goodbye. They pulled away as I watched, drove around the corner of the building, and were gone.

Thirty-Five

Love Conquers All - 2000

"Hello everyone. My name is Richard. I'm not transgender, I'm gay, but I'd like to learn about it. Is it okay to attend your meeting?"

"Of course," we all agreed. It was the first time anyone had come to one of the meetings just to learn.

Richard? There's too many Richards running around here, I mused. Oh, well. He'll probably come to a meeting or two, then go on his way. No big deal.

He was about my height and weight, with glasses and thin blonde hair tied back in a ponytail. A small diamond stud decorated his right ear lobe. It was clear he was interested in our stories, as he listened intently while we went around the room for "check-in." We were all on the same path, but at different stages of the journey. As the evening wore on, the conversation moved to the coming-out process and how families and employers were taking the news, or how we were each preparing for the day we would reveal ourselves.

To our surprise, Richard appeared at the next meeting. He sat on the sofa next to me, and as the evening droned on, he relaxed, putting his arm up on the back of the sofa behind me. About ten minutes into the discussion there was a slight pressure on my neck. I looked over at Richard, who smiled as he proceeded to gently massage my neck and shoulder with his thumb and forefinger.

What the heck! A man was "making advances" on me!

I was dumbfounded. Never in my wildest dreams did I think I'd be in this position. Sure, I had fantasized that I could be made love to by a man, but I never thought it might actually happen.

Oh my gosh, what do I do?

I froze. Richard continued to massage my neck and shoulder for a minute, then casually dropped his hand to his lap. I looked over at him and in a faint, quivering voice whispered, "Thank you."

"You're welcome," he smiled. After the meeting he asked for my phone number.

I gave it to him.

"Hello Erika? It's Richard. Say, I was wondering if I could come over to see your apartment this week. I'll bring a frozen pizza, and we can talk. I've got a few questions I'd like to ask, and I'd rather ask you than the whole group."

"Hi Richard. Umm, sure. How about Saturday? Around six? I'll have ice cream for dessert, if that's all right."

"Okay, Erika. See you then."

I hung up the phone and realized, "Holy shit! I've got a date!"

Richard was prompt. He brought a frozen pizza, as promised, and a bag salad. I added tomatoes to the salad and extra cheese to

248

the pizza and popped it into the oven, then poured us a couple of glasses of wine and sat down.

I wore my favorite brown denim skirt and short-sleeved wool top, with just a light bit of makeup and thin gold necklace to set off the muted colors. My wig was firmly positioned on my head. Worried about what to wear all week, I took solace in the fact he hadn't suggested we go out. He understood from the meetings how terrifying that could be for us. At that moment I was terrified anyway.

"So, can I ask a few questions, Erika?" he began.

"Sure, Richard, go ahead. I'll answer them if I can."

"When did you know you were transgender? Was it when you were young, or later?"

"Well, I had my first cross-dressing experience when I was eight. I didn't know what it was, back then, but I knew it made me feel different to be in girls' clothes. Whole, in a way."

"Was it a sexual experience?"

"Oh, no! It was innocent as all get-out. A neighbor girl and I were playing in her basement one rainy day, and she decided we should play dress-up. We put on clothes her parents were giving to Goodwill, and we role-played all afternoon. She pretended to be married with kids and I pretended to be the manager of a jewelry store."

"Did you do it again?"

"No, but I sure wanted to. It rained the next weekend too, so I asked if she still had the clothes. She didn't—they had taken them to Goodwill. I was devastated," I smiled. "Thus began the long, long road to the here and now."

We talked until the pizza was ready, then ate. Richard was clearly interested in the stories, the whys and the feelings that drove us toward transition.

"As a gay man," he said, "It just scares me to death to think of the surgery you transgenders so desperately want. I mean, being a gay man is all about penises!"

We laughed.

As the evening progressed we became more relaxed with each other and the conversation flowed easily. I asked him about his background, where he grew up, his experience being gay when he was young. It was interesting to see the parallels and differences of our respective journeys. We had finished the first bottle of wine and had popped open the second when he turned to me, a serious look on his face.

"Erika, would it be too much to ask if I could see Rick?"

I paused, thinking furiously to myself. Okay. He's a gay man. He wants to see me as a man. He's been open and honest with me, he's not been pushy or tawdry about it. It's all up front. I should reciprocate, at least this much, just to be fair and open with him.

"Okay, I guess so. I'll have to go upstairs and change, but I'll be back down as soon as I can. Okay?"

He smiled. "No problem. I'll just sit here and drink all your wine."

"I guess I'd better hurry, then."

I went upstairs to take off my Erika clothes and put on Rick's. I chose jeans and a polo shirt, not too casual, not too dressy. Why am I trying to make a good impression? I had no clue. I just didn't want to look like a slob.

I washed off my makeup, put away my earrings and necklace, hung up my skirt and sweater, then turned and stepped hesitantly down the stairs.

"Hello, Rick," Richard said, smiling. "Nice to meet you."

I sat on the sofa and seized my half-empty glass of wine. "Did you leave any for me?" I asked.

"A little," he said, with what I was beginning to see was a characteristic slow smile. He topped off my glass and we sat back to talk, man to man.

We talked for some time, and the evening continued in friendly, open sharing: his experience growing up in small-town Minnesota, mine in big-city Missouri. Our stories were much the same. After a while he moved closer to me, and took my hand.

"Can I kiss you?" he asked softly.

Of course, I knew it was coming. I had practically set it up myself. Now I would find out if I was gay, or if I really wanted to be a woman. Now was truth time.

"Yes, Richard, I think so."

He leaned over, and putting his hand softly on my shoulder, kissed me.

I hadn't expected the feel of mustache hair. He obviously had shaved that day, but a short stubble had already grown on his upper lip. It was scratchy. My gosh, have I got one too? I almost laughed out loud, but held on, suppressing it.

His kiss was soft and full on the lips. A simple kiss, not clutching or grinding, no tongue attacking the back of my throat. It was a respectful kiss, and it was my first. After a long moment he pulled away and looked back at me.

"Are you okay?"

"Yes, I think so. That's my first kiss from a man, so I'm trying to feel my feelings, if you know what I mean. It's difficult."

"Yes, I understand. But don't worry, I won't do anything without your permission. I know this is an important moment for you. I am here, in a way, to help."

Not sure what to do next, I turned and leaned back, nestling myself into his arms. We continued to talk. He occasionally leaned down to kiss my neck, or would caress the back of my head. He was gentle and kind. In due course it was time for a decision.

My heart pounding, I said, "Richard, I'm tired, and would like to go to bed. It's your choice. You can go home, or sleep here on the sofa, or come to bed with me."

He smiled. "I've had too much wine to drive. So, if you're okay with it, I'd like to sleep with you."

I went upstairs first. Standing at my bedroom door, I stopped with the sudden thought: What do I wear? Do I wear my night-gown as usual? It's girly! Underwear? Jeez, this is complicated!

I chose underwear. Men's briefs.

When I was ready, I called down the stairs. "Okay, Richard. Please turn off the lights and come on up."

I jumped into bed and waited, leaning back against the head-board, wondering what the hell I was doing.

Okay. This is it. Am I gay? Am I not gay? Am I both? Neither? Okay, then what am I? Jeez, just admit it. The only thing I know at this moment is that I am scared. I'm just freakin' scared.

A minute later the lights went off downstairs and Richard came up. He walked into the bedroom and smiled at me.

"I'm gonna wash my face. I'll be right back."

He pulled off his shirt and folded it on a chair, then went in to the bathroom. I waited, petrified. When he was done he came back into the bedroom.

"Are you still okay?"

"Yes. I'm scared to death, but I'm okay."

He sat down on the chair and pulled off his shoes, placing them under the chair. Standing, he unbuckled his belt and dropped his jeans to the floor. He didn't take off his underwear, for which I was thankful. I wasn't ready for that quite yet.

He slid under the covers and leaned against the headboard as I had done. I hesitated, then moved over close to him, nestling with my back to him as we had done on the sofa. He put his arm around me, holding me close. We talked a bit more, then he leaned down, kissing me on the cheek.

"Are you ready to lay down?" he asked.

"Yes, I think so."

We lay down, Richard spooning with me from behind. For the first time I felt his erection pressing against my back. His scratchy beard nestled at my neck, his warm wine breath over my shoulder.

It came to me, like a flash, that there was something missing. I did not have an erection myself. My heart was pounding, yes. I had found pleasure in his attentions, his gentleness, yes. But I was not sexually aroused.

No erection. Just terror.

We spooned for a few more minutes, as Richard waited for me to respond. I couldn't. I turned to face him.

"Richard."

"Yes, Rick?"

"I don't think I'm gay."

"Yes, I see that," he sighed, looking down. "Oh, well. I hope I haven't hurt you or offended you in any way. I think too much of you. Can we still be friends?"

"Yes, Richard, I'd like that."

We slept together that night; it was a simple, human sharing of each other's warmth and companionship.

"Rich, why did you get a lawyer? Do you really want a divorce?"

I heard the pain in Barb's voice on the phone. I knew it well. It was my pain too, deep in the middle of my chest, a churning, acid lump.

"Barb, both my shrinks and even some of my friends are saying 'Get a divorce, quick! Get out before your wife eviscerates you in court.' Since we hadn't talked in a while, I thought you had come to the same conclusion."

"Oh my god. I am getting the same advice, Rich. It's horrible. My friends say it, people at work who know what's going on say it. They all do. 'Get a divorce!' they say. But Rich, I've thought about it a lot, and I don't want that. I don't want a divorce. Do you?"

"God, no, Barb! I am overjoyed to hear you say it! I have been torn to pieces by this damn thing, but I don't know what else to do."

After a pause she said quietly, "Why don't you move back to the house? You could take the spare bedroom. It'd be like we were sisters. Is that okay?"

I doubled over in my chair, tears suddenly coming to my eyes. For a long moment, I could not speak.

Then, in a raspy voice, I said, "Yes, yes it is. It sounds very okay."

"It will take me a while to start calling you Erika. I need to adjust, somehow. But I want to try. I really do."

"I understand, Barb, I do. It's okay. I love you."

A short pause, then she spoke. "I love you too…Erika."

It was a chilly Saturday afternoon in the fall. Outside, the sun was yellow-bright, sitting low in the sky, illuminating the multi-colored reds and oranges of maple leaves still on the trees in brilliant splashes of paint waving to every breeze that passed. It was a glorious day, too, in that over the last few weeks Barb and I had fallen back into our old, wonderfully familiar patterns.

We were together again; re-building our lives, yes, but doing it together. Sex was no longer part of our relationship, yet we cared for each other in a way that was stronger now than it had been before. I didn't miss the sex, and Barb was still tentative about physical contact like hugs. That, I hoped, would change with time.

"You need anything at the store?" I asked, thinking about dinner.

"No, I don't think so," Barb replied. "You going anywhere else while you're out?"

"Well, I thought I'd stop by that beauty supply place near the grocery store. I've heard they have the best collection of wigs in town and they're nice to us transgender folks. I need a new wig and thought I'd check them out."

"Would you mind if I came with you?"

"Of course not. That'd be great!"

We walked into the little shop together. I was not dressed as Erika, which made it a bit awkward, but thankfully the place wasn't busy. The nice gray-haired sales lady behind the counter gave us a cheery "Hello! Is there anything I can help you find?" as we walked in. I walked up to the counter.

"We're here to look at wigs," I replied, quietly. "I'm transgender."

"Oh wonderful!" she said happily, in an honest, cheerful way that made it feel like yes, it was wonderful. I looked at Barb, and she was smiling. We both liked her immediately.

"And what style were you thinking of?"

"Well, I tend toward smooth styles, and I think I need one that curves down to hide my jaw line if possible, like a nice bob or page boy. What do you think?"

"Yes. I see you have a squarish kind of facial structure, so that would be a good choice. I've got several in my stock that might suit you, in addition to the ones on display. Why don't you take a look and pick out the ones you like. We've got a nice little private area where you can try them on."

We walked over to a wall of the shop where at least fifty wigs were on display, heads all lined up in row after row. Every style and color imaginable seemed to be there: a bounty of blondes, a bevy of brunettes, a rash of redheads, plus a few greens and purples and pinks, all there.

"Oh my," I said, looking at Barb. "Help!"

She laughed. "Yes, let me help you!"

We walked together down the rows, commenting on this style, that color, figuring out together how best to begin the creation of the new me. Not a brash, in-your-face Erika, we agreed, but an

Erika with class. A professional Erika, an educated woman with a sense of style and clear purpose in life. A woman who accepts herself, and is accepted by the love of her life, the woman walking beside her in the wig store. We picked a nice layered page-boy bob in light brown with blonde highlights.

Barb bought the wig for me.

TRANS-FORMATIONS

Thirty-Six

Our Parents - 2000

The phone rang. It was late, so I picked up quickly, so as to not wake Barb in her bedroom.

"Mr. Logan?"

Who would be calling for "Logan" at this hour?

"No, my wife's last name is Logan. Mine is Shepard."

"Okay. Mr. Shepard, this is Detective Duncan with the Portland police department. Do you know Wyatt Logan?"

"Yes, he's my father-in-law." Portland? What the heck? Wyatt lives near Seattle!

"Mr. Shepard, your father-in-law has been detained. He's not under arrest, but he is exhibiting rather erratic behavior, and he's being held as a possible danger to himself or others. Your number was in his wallet as an emergency contact."

"Oh my gosh! What kind of behavior!?"

"At approximately eight this evening he called 911 from a convenience store, claiming people were after him and he was in danger. A patrol car responded, and found him armed with a .45 caliber military pistol. His car was loaded with all sorts of odds and ends plus his little dog. It appeared to the responding officers that he was suffering from some kind of impairment—they thought it might be dementia—so they calmed him down, disarmed him, and took him to the psychiatric ward of the local hospital for evaluation. I can give you the contact information at the hospital and the convenience store where his car is still parked. It's safe for now. Do you have pen and paper handy?"

"Ready."

The detective recited the information.

"Thank you sir. What about the dog?"

"Mr. Logan was attached to the dog, so the officers and staff at the hospital thought it best to let the dog stay with him for the time being, to keep him calm."

"That's a relief. Anything else I need to know?"

"You should get down here as soon as you can to meet with the hospital staff and retrieve the car. He was admitted on a seventy-two hour evaluation."

"Thanks again, detective."

"You're welcome. By the way, is it true he's an ex-cop and war hero?"

"Yes sir, it is. Twenty years with the Kansas City police force, and career Army before that. He earned a silver star and battlefield commission in Korea."

"Damn. It's always sad when these kind of things happen. If you need anything from us, just contact me. He's one of our own and we'll do what we can for him."

"Will do, sir. Thank you."

Wyatt was admitted to a memory care facility in Olympia, Washington. Barb's younger sister Sue and her husband lived nearby and would handle things, visiting him more often than we could. Plus we all agreed: if Wyatt found out about me, he would want to kill me.

⤳

"Hello, Erika? This is Brenda."

It was not good news. Mom had begun suffering mini-strokes. She had been transported to the hospital, where the doctors determined that her digestive system was compromised and not functioning properly. There was pain.

Early Saturday morning, I hit the road. It was an eleven-hour drive to Brenda's town on the Oregon coast, and I wanted to be there before visiting hours ended, and perhaps be able to talk with Mom's doctors. I went as Rick. Mom had enough on her plate without Erika showing up at her hospital room door.

Traffic through Seattle was light, so I made good time, but Portland was a mess. A bit south of Corvallis it lightened up, however, and I was able to pin the needle five miles an hour above the limit. All was well until about ten minutes past the last exit to Medford. My cell phone, lying in the seat beside me, rang.

I fumbled to pick up the phone. "Hello?"

"Rich, it's Barb. Something's happened. Sue called, and Dad has been admitted to the ICU in Olympia. The Alzheimer's has gotten bad and they don't know how much longer he's going to last. Can you come? Where are you? I'll meet you there."

"Oh, shit. Yes, I'll turn around as soon as I can. I'm south of Medford, so it will take me a several hours to get back to Olympia. Do you have the name of the hospital?" I kept on driving, listening carefully. Luckily, there was a rest stop a few miles ahead. I stopped there to call Brenda and see how Mom was doing.

"So, Brenda, that's my problem. Wyatt may be dying, and Barb needs me. Is Mom stable? I hate to do it, but I've got to make a choice. If Wyatt is more critical, I'll go there. If Mom is the same or worse, I'll keep coming."

"Mom is doing okay, so I don't think you need to come here right away. They're talking about letting her out of the hospital in a day or two, depending on how she responds."

"Okay, then I'll turn around and head back to Olympia. As soon as I know the status of things there, I'll call you."

I pulled out of the rest area and continued south toward the foothills of the Klamath Mountains. I knew from previous trips that there was no exit to turn around for at least twenty miles.

Behind me, the nearest traffic was a couple of miles away. Ahead of me, in the oncoming direction, was a single truck that would pass me in less than a minute. Behind it was a big gap until the next vehicle.

As soon as the truck on the other side of the road passed, I slowed abruptly, then angled across the grassy median strip, dust billowing in a cloud behind me.

I pulled into the northbound lane, accelerating.

"Goddammit!"

Barb and I, sleeping in the hospital chairs in Wyatt's room, jumped, awakened in the semi-darkness. He hadn't said a word in the twelve or so hours we had been there, remaining comatose and unresponsive, unaware of his surroundings.

I scrambled to the head of his bed and flipped on the overhead light. Wyatt was lying there, eyes closed, breathing tubes in his nose still in place. It was as if we had dreamed it. I looked over at Barb who had come to the other side of the bed.

"What the...?"

"He's still out of it? My god, he's still asleep or whatever! Where did that come from?" Barb shook her head. "He's gonna be a pain in the ass all the way to the end, isn't he," she said.

"Yeah, sure looks like it."

"What time is it?"

"By my watch it's about three in the morning."

"Well, I can't get back to sleep now. Why don't you go get us some coffee? Sue should be back in three or four hours, and we can decide what to do then."

"Okay," I said. "I'll get us some stale little chocolate donuts too, if there's any left in the vending machine."

"Oh, joy," she replied with a straight face. It had been a long twelve hours.

Wyatt remained quiet, unmoving for the next few hours until Barb's sister arrived. They went off to have a conference with the doctor while I stayed in the room. I couldn't hear Wyatt's breathing, but his chest moved with each breath. He was wired into a monitor that stood on a stand next to his bed. It made no sound, offering only thin green squiggles on a small black screen to show he was still alive. The nurse came in to check his IV drip. She just smiled at me and went about her business. She'd seen it all before.

After a time, Barb and Sue came back to the room. "Why don't you go down to the lounge area and try to get some sleep, Rich," Barb said. "We'll stay here for a while."

"Okay. I'll be back in an hour or so. Come get me if you need anything."

Bleary-eyed, I made my way down to the main lobby of the hospital. It was still early morning, and there were couches there that I could stretch out on. I found one near the back wall, and lay down. It seemed like moments later when Barb was standing over me, shaking me awake.

"Wake up Rich. Wake up. It's over."

I sat up. She had been crying.

"It's over?"

"Yeah. He just stopped. He didn't struggle, he didn't swear out loud any more, he just stopped. The monitor beeped a few times, and that was it. He was DNR, so they just let it happen. There's nothing they could have done anyway. It's over."

"Oh, sweetie, I'm so sorry." I stood and took her into my arms. She leaned her head down, putting it on my shoulder. She felt stiff, rigid at first, then, slowly, she relaxed as I held her. I felt her tears soaking through my shirt. We stood together, holding each other, sharing our sadness.

Two hours later, I was on the road again, speeding south to Oregon, mind racing as fast as the car.

Both of Barb's parents were gone now. My mother was sliding away. Soon we both would become orphans, in a way. Just us. Next in line. It was a disturbing feeling of mortality.

But I was grateful that we were together to face it.

The doctors released Mom from the hospital the day after I arrived. They had managed to quell the mini-strokes with blood thinners, and her digestive tract had started back up, at least in part. They added strong laxatives to her medication list. She was not amused, but she was stable and could function, so she was transferred back to her assisted-living facility.

I returned to Bellingham to pick up where I had left off, planning my coming out at work. "D-Day" I called it: Disclosure Day.

A few weeks later I received another call from Brenda. Mom was back in the hospital, and it didn't look good.

By now I knew the way to Brenda's place almost in my sleep—I knew where the slow parts were, what lane to be in when the interstate narrowed for an obligatory exit, where the cops might be hiding. What had taken me eleven and a half hours the first time, now took ten and a half. Still, it was a long drive, my mind grappling with the reality of what was happening to our mother.

When I arrived, it was clear that she was in a bad way. Her abdomen was bloated, despite the ministrations of the doctor. Brenda and I stayed in the room and held Mom's hands as the doctor tried to manually remove as much of the obstruction in her bowel as possible. The results were awful—the terrible pain, the smell, the indignity. It was dreadful for everyone.

When the doctor and Brenda had left the room, I stayed behind, holding Mom's hand. She laid back, eyes closed, tears streaking her cheeks. Gazing at her in the hospital bed, there were dark circles under her eyes. Her face had a grayish tint, a sunken look.

Time is short, I realized.

She opened her eyes and turned to me seated beside her. With great effort, she reached over to me with her good hand. Grabbing my shirt sleeve, she pulled me close. I saw pain in her eyes, smelled her sour breath. She said nothing, but I could see—she had had enough. She couldn't endure any more suffering. She wanted me to make it stop.

Please, she was saying, make it stop.

"Okay, Mom, I understand. No more. No more pain. It stops now. I love you, Mom. It stops now."

She let go of my arm and fell back to the bed.

It was up to me now.

She closed her eyes. After a few minutes I slipped out of the room. Brenda was sitting in the waiting area at the end of the hall. I walked down the long corridor and sat down beside her.

"What did the doctor say, Brenda?"

"He said there's nothing more they can do. They've tried everything."

"Yeah. I think that's about right. And Mom can't take any more."

"I don't think she can either."

"While you were out of the room she grabbed me. She let me know, in her own way, that she's had enough. She wants to end this."

"Oh."

"Yeah."

"So, just to make sure I got it right, will you go talk to her about it? Can you do that?"

"Okay." Brenda paused, then stood and made her way down to Mom's room. I got up and stepped over to the nurses' station.

"Could you call the doctor for us? Our mother can't take any more of this. We'd like to talk with him about hospice or palliative care."

Mom passed away in her sleep at Brenda's house two days later.

The next day we made the arrangements. We called our sister Barbara and arranged for her and her daughter to fly from Kansas City. We spoke with the town mortuary about Mom's service and cremation. We were numb, going through the motions required of us.

Mom was gone. It seemed unreal.

I drove to a local beach, trying to compose a suitable obituary and a short service as I walked across the sand listening to the waves. Occasionally, I found a nice rock to sit on and cry. There were few people on the beach to witness the spectacle.

Brenda and I had talked about it, and we decided to have Mom in a side viewing room during the service. Behind us in the main room we placed a table. On it we put a big picture of Mom, and few of her treasured items: some of her cherished silver and turquoise jewelry and her pilot's logbook. Among the keepsakes were three long-stemmed red roses, one to represent each of us kids. I cobbled together a music selection, classical mostly, from Mom's collection, to be played in the background. It would have been what Mom wanted, we thought.

We held it on a Sunday. It lasted less than an hour.

On Monday morning, I waited for the funeral home to deliver Mom's ashes. Brenda didn't want to keep them, so I agreed take them home with me for the time being while Brenda's husband made arrangements to scatter Mom's ashes at sea. He had a connection with the Coast Guard, and because Mom had been a flight instructor for young men who went to war and an officer in the Civil Air Patrol, they were happy to grant her last honors.

I returned to the beach where I had written Mom's obituary. Again, there were few people about, so I wandered southward, walking in the strand line where the sand was firmest. Three-foot waves crashed against the offshore rocks scattered in the bay, throwing great frothy sprays of seawater into the wind. I felt the salty mist on my face, tasted it on my lips. Head down, I walked at a slow pace for a long time, aware of the continuous sound they made, each wave adding its part to an incohesive roar. I let the sound fill my head. I did not think. I just walked, just breathed, carefully exploring the ragged new hole in my heart.

About a mile south of the parking area, a young woman appeared walking around the tip of a little spit of land, coming toward me. As we approached, we greeted each other.

"There's a little cove about a quarter mile back," she said, smiling. "People have been making art from found objects on a sand dune. It's worth a look."

"Thanks, I'll check it out." With that we continued on our respective ways.

It was a nice spot. The little cove tended to be a place where trash, driftwood, and seaweed collected, tossed there by the sea, but it was surprisingly quiet compared to the long beach behind me. I sat for a while, then decided what to do. I collected three short logs of straight driftwood and planted them upright in the sand, shoulder to shoulder, but at different heights. I then wrapped them together in a length of seaweed. On top of each I balanced a pebble, one for each of us. My pebble was of two rock types melted together in some ancient magmatic intrusion, one side gray, one side white. It seemed fitting.

When it was done, I turned and walked back the way I had come, again with my head down. Soon I encountered my own tracks in the sand, but no others. The woman who had told me about the cove was long gone.

It was so hard to believe. Mom was dead. Mom, the pilot, the rebel, a strong woman who raised three kids pretty much alone. She'd had a difficult life, and now she was gone.

I wished I had been more attentive to her before the stroke, a better "son," perhaps. Who knew? I might have been a good daughter as well. I had so many questions I wished I had asked, but the stroke and now her death had stolen that chance away. I missed it, because I was too busy, or working somewhere far away, or just too stupid.

Mom, I'm so sorry. I'm so sorry I wasn't a good son.

Through the tears, I became aware of something just at the edge of my field of vision: an object, washing ashore in the waves. I stepped to the shallow water to see what it was.

It was a long-stemmed red rose.

It was alone on the beach, rolling back and forth in the shallow water. No flotsam or trash or driftwood was with it, just the rose, intact. Twenty yards off shore, crashing surf pounded against rocky outcrops strewn across the water like castle guards. Yet here was a fragile blossom, unbroken, all petals in place, the color rich and vibrant.

I couldn't pick it up. I just stared. As if in a trance, I turned and walked to a nearby rock and collapsed. I melted, I sobbed, I rocked back and forth in my grief.

Mom, oh Mom, Thank you for this, thank you for all you did. Your courage saved my life. Wherever you are, thank you.

TRANS-FORMATIONS

Thirty-Seven

D-Day - 2001

"In the Case of Richard James Shepard, regarding a name change, all parties come forward."

We stood, my friend from the support group and I. Today, I would officially become Erika Jean Shepard. Richard would be no more.

I wore my new business suit, a simple black collarless blazer with matching straight skirt and a satin camisole in beige to set it off. One of Barb's thin gold necklaces hung from my neck. I had small gold studs in my ears. I wore the wig Barb had bought for me. I had applied makeup lightly, as I wanted to appear business-like, as if I had my act together.

"You're Richard Shepard?" the judge asked when I approached.

"Yes sir."

He paused a moment, then looked down at the papers in front of him.

"All right. Do you swear that you are not seeking to change your name for fraudulent reasons, that you are not a convicted felon under supervision of the Department of Corrections, nor a registered sex offender, and that the change of name will not be detrimental to the interests of any other persons?"

"Yes sir, I do."

"Then the court hereby rules your petition is accepted and shall become part of the record."

He then looked up at me and smiled. "Ms. Erika Jean Shepard, I wish you the best of luck in your new life."

"Thank you sir. Thank you!"

Disclosure Day.

Although I had been planning it for months and had high hopes for my success, I knew the culture at the mill was that of an old-boys network in the South. Pocket protectors and cheap poly-ester ties were the uniform, and no women occupied any part of senior management that I had seen. But I was ready, or so I hoped.

I had assembled three copies of an information packet. They each contained a cover letter outlining my intent to come to work as Erika on the first day of work, 2001, plus general information about transgenderism. I included a complete list of my customers, highlighting those that I had met face-to-face as Rick. I included copies of the section of the Human Resources Manual that dis-cussed discrimination, including sex discrimination and harass-ment.

The final page was a copy of a recent memo from the CEO. It stated, in no uncertain terms, that the company would not dis-criminate on the basis of "sexual orientation" in their hiring or treatment of employees. I hoped this last, which had been distrib-uted just a few months before, might give my bosses pause as they scrambled for a reason to fire me.

I gave one packet to my boss. I gave the second packet to his boss. I gave the third to the head of HR.

Then I went to the bathroom and threw up.

There was a knock at my office door early the next day.

"Hi, Tom." My boss. He looked nervous.

"Uh, good morning, Rick. Can we talk for minute?"

"Of course. Have a seat."

He sat down, quickly crossing his legs and folding his arms over his chest. "Well, we're trying to wrap our heads around the information you gave us yesterday."

"I understand. I'm open to any questions you might want to ask, believe me."

"Thanks, perhaps a bit later. Right now we want to ask you not to discuss this with anyone here at the company. We've contacted the head office, and they've referred it to the Legal Department. In the meantime, we're not supposed to discuss it with you or any-one."

"How long do you think they will take?"

"It's hard to say, but I expect we will hear from them by the end of the week."

"Okay, Tom, no problem. I want to be as cooperative as I can on this."

"Thanks, Rick, I appreciate it. One more thing: we especially don't want you to talk to any of your customers about it. Okay?"

"Okay, Tom."

"Thanks," he said, then scurried away.

Well, they're nervous, that much is clear, I thought. They've contacted the corporate Legal Department, which means my fate is in their hands. Oh, well. I'm ready. I already know which lawyers I'm going to call if this all goes south.

"So Rick, the company is planning to do a couple of things in preparation for your first day at work as, uh, Erika," Tom said. He was nervous again.

"What's the plan, Tom?"

"We're going to hold an office meeting next week to an-nounce it to the entire staff. We would prefer it if you did not at-tend. Second, we will draft a letter to your customers explaining the change, offering them the opportunity to work with a differ-ent sales representative if they so choose. And third, we're setting aside a bathroom for you to use. It's on the third floor in the back of the Lab building."

I pondered the plan Tom had outlined for a long moment, letting the silence wear on him a bit. So. They want to control the narrative, both here in the office and with my customers. They also would prefer to dodge the "bathroom issue" by sending me to the outer edge of the paper mill universe to pee. Separate but equal? Just paint over the "Colored" sign, if you please.

On the other hand, I could keep my job—probably. I'll bet they expect most or all of my customers to ask for new represen-tation, giving them a reason to fire me, I realized. Not their fault, they'll say. Meanwhile, I'll be treated like I've got the plague. Oh, well. I knew this would not go smoothly.

"Okay, Tom, I understand. I'll meet you halfway. I want the right to edit that letter to the customers before it goes out, and I want you to read a statement from me to everyone at the meeting. I'll not fuss about the bathroom. I expected as much. Does that work for you?"

"I'll talk to the others, but I think that will be just fine. Thank you, Rick."

"You're welcome, Tom. And please, come January, my name is Erika."

I was surprised. Thirteen people came by my office after the meeting to say they supported me. None of my clients asked for a different sales representative, and two went so far as to call me personally to voice their support. The problem was, my boss and several co-workers wanted nothing to do with me. Two of them found ways to insult me to my face at meetings and in public.

It was just a month after D-Day when I and two of those co-workers, Bob and Brian, were sent to Denver for a convention of the Society of Mining Engineers. I was tasked with finding a way to supply our products to the mining industry. Bob and Brian sold products for dust suppression on gravel roads. They were a couple of good ol' boys, and were not happy sitting in a convention booth with me. They made themselves scarce when I had booth duty.

The third night of the four-day convention, they grudgingly agreed to have dinner together in a downtown restaurant.

"So, I don't get it. Why the hell are ya doing this?" Bob asked over his third beer. 'Ya know, no matter what, it's a selfish thing to do. Just selfish."

"More than that," piped in Brian, "it's just emotional. You know all emotions come from the base brain, the reptile brain, and so what you're doing is stupid. You gotta ignore it and listen to your higher brain."

They went at me like a tag team, harder and harder, louder and louder, drunker and drunker. People at other tables were turning their heads in irritation. I tried to explain that it wasn't emotional, it was physical and psychological and I didn't just make it up, but I was never allowed to finish a sentence. They just hammered away.

I finally fell apart. I began to cry. Quietly, staring down at the remains of my dinner, in a fancy downtown Denver restaurant, I cried.

I complained to the HR department when we got back. It made no difference. I still had the plague.

In the long run it didn't matter. Six months later the plant was closed, in large part due to the energy crisis precipitated by the Enron Corporation.

Once again, I found myself unemployed—but this time, as Erika.

Thirty-Eight

Survival and Hope - 2002

I renewed my search for employment as geologist again, most-ly with exploration and mining companies based in Vancouver, B.C. Yet month after month, there was no response. There were jobs, but they went to Canadian geologists. So I widened my search to include anything and everything. Finally, I got an interview with a cell phone company, at a large call center in town.

"We pay eleven dollars an hour, to start," the very young HR representative said. "We offer health insurance and paid time off after one year. The first six weeks you'd be in training, and if you miss two or more training days you will be dropped from the program. After a year you'll be eligible for a raise if your statistics are good."

"What are the hours?" I asked.

"They vary. You'll be working with a team of ten others and a supervisor, and the team works the same shift. The call center is open from five a.m. to eleven p.m., so your shift could be any time in that range. New hires like yourself usually end up with the early shifts."

"I see." An early shift would leave me free in the afternoons to go to interviews and such, I thought.

"One other question. Is there any problem with me being transgender?"

"No, of course not!" She actually blushed. "We're an equal opportunity employer, so no problem."

"Are there any other transgender people working here?"

"Not that I know of. But it wouldn't be a problem."

"Okay. I think I'd like to apply, if possible."

"Oh, good!" She slid an application form across the desk to me. "Just fill this out, then we'll go in the next room for your typing test. You've got to type forty words a minute to qualify."

I made it, barely.

It was shift work in a call center: two acres of gray, featureless cubicles lined up row after row, inhabited by haunted figures bent over computer screens, headsets clamped to their skulls, like unhappy robots all forced to make a living. It was the reality version of *The Matrix*.

When I first walked in the door, I had not realized that it wasn't a customer service center for the company—it was collections. If a customer with a past due bill tried to make a call, it was automatically routed to us to collect on the bill. Each call was timed to the second, and our collections were totaled on an hourly basis. I had never before worked in such a rigid environment, even in the Navy.

The company tried to make it bearable, within limits. There was a "Relaxation Room," a retreat off to one side of the cavernous main floor, complete with Zen music and videos of seashores. It was a place to hide on your break when the stress got too bad. Nevertheless, the center was not a humane place.

Worse, I found that if I used my real name on the calls—Erika—I'd end up spending precious time explaining my personal life to total strangers. My voice was masculine, and it threw them off. The company said I could do whatever I wanted, but I needed to improve my scores. In desperation I began using "Erik." It felt strange saying it. Not my name, dammit, not my name.

My statistics improved a bit, but I still wasn't good at it.

"So, tell me, Erika, what kind of woman would you like to be?" Dr. Krympe asked. "You've thought about it, I expect. What is the ideal for you?"

"Well, yes I have, of course. Mostly I'd like to pass as a woman. Just an ordinary, unremarkable woman that looks like Michelle Pfeiffer or maybe Jodie Foster."

"You're not the only one!" she laughed. "So, a career woman? A housewife, a secretary, a female geologist? What is the ideal vision for yourself that you have in mind?"

"Okay, the ideal vision. I see myself able to pass as a woman, not remarkable, just another woman in the grocery store checkout line, or walking across a parking lot. And I would love to get back into geology. I miss it: the excitement, the challenge, just the plain joy of it. What I'm doing now just sucks. I don't want to be stuck in a call center the rest of my life, nor do I want to be buried in a similar job elsewhere, just part of the machinery."

"What about relationships? What about Barb?"

"Yeah, that. Well, Barb and I are best friends. But I miss, as I'm sure she does, the intimacy of a regular marriage, of what we had before, however flawed it might have been. Simply sleeping together, sharing a warm cuddle on a cold, rainy morning, is gone. We don't relate that way anymore, and, well, it hurts."

"I see. And...?"

"If you're asking if I will try to find love somewhere else, the answer is no. I can't see the love we have ever happening again, certainly not for me."

"We're talking the ideal here, but if you could change things with Barb, what would it be? More intimacy, as you describe?"

"Yes, I guess so. She is not a lesbian, and we have too much history with me as Rich for her to ever be comfortable, I expect. It's one thing when your lover has a hard-on, quite another when they have bigger boobs than you."

"And you are willing to live with that?"

"Yes, I am. You asked me about my ideal life, but I now understand the physical part of it was an unrealistic fantasy all along. No matter how much surgery I get, I'll never look like Michelle Pfeiffer. I'll always have a low voice. I'll never quite pass."

"Does that bother you?"

"You know, Dr. Sandra, trying to change myself, my looks, how I sound, would have required extensive surgery on my face, my voice. Yet I'd simply have turned myself into a distorted version of Jodie or Michelle at best. I've come to realize it would be just another version of living up to other people's expectations.

"As I've moved along, though, I've become more and more comfortable with who I am. That's a surprise to me in all of this. A welcome surprise. So I'll just try to be the best woman I can be, and deal with whatever comes my way, good or bad. I think, after all that I've gone through, that I will be just fine."

"So then, how do you see the specifics of your life going forward? What are you going to do with your new life, however it unfolds?"

"Well, I see it going forward with Barb, as long as she'll have me. I see getting back into geology again, somewhere, somehow. I'm still applying for exploration jobs. I see us in twenty years still living together, perhaps with a bit more intimacy, perhaps not. I've even thought about writing a book someday.

"After retirement, I'd love it if Barb and I traveled to some of the places I've worked. There's some amazing spots I'd like to show her. Beyond that, I haven't a clue. I've also learned through all of this that plans are fragile things."

"But you have hope?"

"Yes, I have hope."

TRANS-FORMATIONS

Thirty-Nine

An Ordinary Woman - 2002

I waited until she got home. I didn't want to call her at the office with this kind of news.

"Barb. I got a call from Montreal today. I have a surgery date."

She froze, shock and dread on her face. We had talked about it. But until now, this moment, it had always seemed unreal, a far-off event that might not ever occur.

"When is it?"

"I fly to Montreal on October 10th, with surgery on the 15th. I return on the 24th."

Another pause, then: "I can't get that much time off from work, I'm sure. So I can't come with you. I'm sorry, but I just can't."

"That's okay, sweetie, I understand."

"I thought I wanted to come, and I want to support you, but it's hard for me, you know? It'd be hard for me to go there, knowing what it means, what's going to happen. It's too final."

"I understand. It's scary and hard for me too. And yet...."

"Yes. You have to do it. I understand that now. It hurts, though. It hurts."

283

❧

We stood next to the car in front of the Vancouver airport departure area. It was cold, the wind whipping through the crowded lanes behind us. We faced each other, both near tears as we tried to maintain control, to hold off the overwhelming need to start weeping right there.

"I love you, sweetie," I said, voice cracking.

"I love you too," she responded, her voice broken as well. "Can you have someone call me after the surgery? I want to know that you're all right."

"Of course. I'll get one of the nurses to do it, or someone else who's there."

We kissed. A brief kiss, one that meant goodbye at so many levels. Then Barb turned and quickly got back into the car. At that moment, it was finally real. She was losing her husband. No chance he would come back now.

I turned and, dragging my bag, walked into the airport.

Sitting at the gate, I tried to make sense of it all. I felt a profound sadness, somehow mixed with intense anticipation. Like Barb, I was losing Richard too, although I had given him up years ago. Our marriage had been tested beyond ordinary measure, and survived. But it had changed. It was still changing. I had hope— even faith—that a better, happier relationship would emerge from all the pain.

It seemed unreal. A lifetime, a million tears, a thousand painful moments, and now I was there, on the brink, leaping over that cliff again. I wouldn't be hiding any more. The girl in the mirror would be me, for better or worse.

Would my life be as I first envisioned? Absolutely not. The pipe dreams were long gone. But I thought I understood what my new reality would be—our new reality, Barb and me. I wouldn't be alone. She wouldn't be alone. Together, we could face anything.

And it was her courage that had made it possible.

"Hello, I'm Erika," I said to the man at the gate holding a sign with my name on it.

"Eerika Sheepard?" he asked in a beautiful French-Canadian accent. I almost answered, "Oui, monsieur."

"Yes sir, that's right."

"Ah, bien. I am your driver. My name is Robert." He pronounced it *Ro-bear*. "I am to take you to the Residence."

"Oh, thank you. I wasn't expecting to be met at the airport."

"Ees no problem. I meet most of Dr. Brassard's clients here."

With that, he took my bag and turned toward the terminal door. I followed him to a black limousine parked at the curb, where he held the rear door open for me. He then loaded my bag into the trunk and we were off.

It was a sunny fall afternoon in Montreal. The freeway was like any other, but soon we turned off and began to wend our way through the quaint neighborhoods of the city. Maples arched over the streets, glowing in their autumn colors, gaudy splashes of orange and red, set off by the velvety browns of somber oaks, all painted against a thick backdrop of evergreens of every variety. Crisp and beautiful, there was a welcome feeling to the air.

We turned down a narrow lane, crossing an old stone bridge. Beneath us passed a wide, shallow creek lined with bright pebbles and boulders, rippled with silver-clear water. Over the short bridge, we glided down a curved driveway to the front door of The Residence.

The Residence was a large mansion on an island on the north shore of a tributary to the St. Lawrence River. The large property was a mix of well-tended grass, flower gardens, and a small beach with a quaint wooden shelter overlooking the water.

Inside, I noted that the entry to the Mansion was paved with local flagstones—a nice mica schist. The walls were stucco white, interspersed with rough-hewn oak beams extending up to the high ceiling where more beams were exposed. A large round chandelier hung from a beam over a living room area complete with stone fireplace. Several people were sitting in the comfortable-looking chairs, talking among themselves or reading, enjoying the fire.

I signed in at a small desk next to the door, and the attendant handed me a key.

"Here is your room key, Miss Shepard. You are on the second floor overlooking the patio on the south side of the building. Robert will take your bags up, so please just make yourself comfortable. Tea, coffee, and juice are available on the table by the kitchen. Dinner is at six in the dining room."

I stepped over to the table and poured myself a glass of orange juice, then walked over to the group by the fire.

"Hello, everyone. My name is Erika."

We made introductions all around. Some of them were like me, scheduled for surgery in a few days. Others had had their surgeries three days earlier and were recovering.

"The doctor will be here on Monday," they said. "That's when he checks on those of us who have had surgery, and interviews those who are scheduled next. Meanwhile, we just hang around here or go shopping in town. Have you seen the indoor pool and hot tub yet?"

Wait two more days until we know if we could have the surgery? Oh, well, I thought. Hot tub, fireplace, and meals cooked for us. It wouldn't be all bad. Plus I could ask them how it went, how they feel, what to look forward to. They seemed open to questions, like me. After all, no matter where we came from, we shared a common bond, a similar struggle.

"So, Erika, welcome to Montreal. Have you been here before?"

"No, Dr. Brassard, I haven't. The small part I've seen is just beautiful, though."

Dr. Brassard was perhaps forty, a tall man with dark, curly hair, blue eyes, and a quick, engaging smile. We sat across from each other in soft leather chairs on a landing of the stairway to the second floor. It was a comfortable space, with shelves bearing books behind the chairs and antique floor lamps beside each one. Outside, the weather had changed to rain, but even with the wet gray skies hanging over the tall windows, the space had a warmth to it. I would gladly have sat in the chair, bathed in a pool of warm light from the old floor lamp, reading a good book—except that, at the moment, my future existence was being decided. Except for that....

"Yes, as cities go," he continued, "it's a special place. If you get the chance, go to the downtown district, the Old City. This time of year the fall colors are quite beautiful."

"Thanks, I might try to go tomorrow then, before surgery."

"Yes, that would be good."

287

"Well, now, let's see." He opened the thick file folder in his lap. "All your paperwork is here, and you appear to be in good physical health. So. I don't see any medical reason that bars you from surgery."

He closed the folder. Then looking me in the eye, he said, "That leads to my first and most important question. Are you ready for this?"

Can a life be squeezed into one moment? Can a single decision, a single word, determine your destiny? Did I have the courage, after all, to go forward with this?

"Yes."

The word escaped from my mouth almost of its own accord, welling up from a deep place I had spent most of my lifetime denying. It was me saying it, and it was that girl. That girl in me who had been trapped for a lifetime, hiding, ashamed of her very existence. That girl I had released from her prison as much as I could. She now stood at the threshold of a new life. Just one more step, that's all. Just one more. She craved freedom, and in her freedom I would attain my own. No longer hidden behind my eyes, no longer afraid.

She is me, and I am her. As it always has been. Yes.

Dr. Brassard then asked a few questions about breast implants. I could choose the size of my breasts, he said. He reminded me that I would have to take hormones for the rest of my life and that my neo-vagina would require painful weekly maintenance for it to remain open.

"Yes," I responded, still in a daze. "I'm prepared for that."

"All right, Erika," he finally said, smiling, "I will see you Wednesday morning at the surgical center. If you have any questions, just have the staff call me. Bien?"

❧

Dr. Brassard's small surgical hospital was in another part of town, so Robert and his limo were called into service. He loaded four of us up on Tuesday afternoon after a light lunch. We would not eat again until after the surgery.

Among the group were another transgender woman from Montana, Alice, and her mother, Diane, who had come to support her. We talked of small things along the way, the wonderful fall colors, how cold it was back home right now, the rains in Washington State, anything but the implications of the next 24 hours.

We checked in and were ushered to our room. I was given the bed by the window, a bright yellow-orange maple tree just outside.

I called Barb that night.

"Hi, sweetie."

"Hi. How are you?" I heard the tension in her voice, and the sadness.

"I'm fine, I'm at the hospital, but they're starving us. No dinner for the guilty, it seems. Something about having clean innards," I said, trying to make small talk.

"Yeah, that makes sense."

"Are you doing okay?"

"Yeah, I'll be okay. I wish I could be there with you. You know that, don't you?"

"Absolutely, I know. By the way, I'll be taken to surgery about one o'clock. They'll call you after I get out to let you know I'm all right. That'll be mid-afternoon your time, so they might call at work. Is that all right?

"Yes, I'll want to know. So call me when you can after the surgery, okay?"

"Of course."

There was nothing else to say. We said our loving goodbyes and hung up.

ॐ

Alice was taken first to the surgery the next morning. Meanwhile, I tried to relax, listening to classical music on headphones, staring out the window, my mind racing in a thousand directions at once.

They came for me about 1 p.m.

"Your turn!" the lead nurse said in a cheerful voice as they wheeled Alice into the room with her mother close behind.

My turn. I transferred to another gurney, and out we went.

We rolled onto an elevator and rose up one level. They wheeled me into a large room, white tile walls and various medical devices arranged around the perimeter. It was cold, and the white light from the overhead fluorescents made it feel even colder.

The face of a doctor I had not met appeared over me.

"Hello, Erika. I'm the anesthesiologist, Dr. Purdue. Have you had anesthesia administered before?"

"Yes sir, I have."

"Any problems?"

"No sir, no problems at all."

"Excellent. So then, we will proceed like this; I will give you a small injection before we go into the operating room. It will make you sleepy, but you will not become unconscious. Once you are in position, I will administer the actual anesthetic. After surgery, you will wake up in your room. Is this clear?"

"Yes sir, all clear."

"Okay. Dr. Brassard will be in to see you in a moment."

Just a minute or so later, Dr. Brassard's face appeared.

"Hello, Erika, how are you?"

"I'm fine, Dr. Brassard, at least I think so."

"Yes, it's like that," he smiled. "I understand. So then, I will ask you one more time. Are you ready for this?"

"Yes sir, I am." No pause, no regrets. Just yes.

"That is good. We will see you in the operating room in a few minutes, then." With that he walked away.

Dr. Purdue returned with a syringe and gave me the shot. A warm, soft blanket came over me. He then set up an IV with a clear fluid, inserting the needle in my right arm near my thumb, securing it with white tape. He smiled and left. A minute later two nurses appeared and wheeled me into the operating room.

It was a small room with white tile walls like the first room. Equipment was placed along the walls and next to the operating table in the center. There was classical music playing in the background. Bach? I wondered. No, but certainly baroque. For some reason it made me feel peaceful, relaxed. It was reassuring proof I was in good hands.

They positioned me next to the table and held the gurney while I awkwardly slid over onto it, the nurses helping me. When I was in position, one of them came around the bed and installed stirrups at the foot of the table. I'm about to get my first pelvic exam, I thought. It was funny in a dream-like way. I smiled at Dr. Brassard, and he smiled back through his mask.

Dr. Purdue sat down in a chair to the left of me near my head, while Dr. Brassard sat in a rolling chair between my elevated legs. Then Dr. Purdue looked down and put his hand on my shoulder.

"Are you ready, Erika?"

I nodded, then lost consciousness.

Awareness came slowly as I emerged from a soft, dreamless place. I was lying on my back, looking up at an acoustical tile ceiling.

Back in the room, I thought dreamily. Okay, that means it's done. Do I feel any different? Ugh, the only thing I feel right now is pain. Pain in my crotch and my bloated gut, pain on my chest.

Chest. That must be my boobs.

I raised my right arm and felt the IV line restrict it, so I moved my left, bringing it to my chest. I felt nothing but a mass of gauze bandages and tape over my chest, hot and uncomfortable. But I knew; the pain meant I had breasts.

My breasts. My boobs, I marveled. My girls. Mine.

What about below? Extending my arm, I found that that, too, was a great wad of gauze and tape that extended all the way down and, as I began to realize, up inside me. I was packed up tight, top and bottom. It meant that I no longer had a penis. I had a vagina.

The realization enveloped me, folding itself around me. It was validation of identity, profound beyond my greatest imaginings. I had breasts. I had a vagina. I was now female.

I felt an all-encompassing warmth at the thought, a warmth that flooded through me, reaching every corner of my being. The twisted pain I had endured all of my life was gone, replaced by a feeling of connection, by an awareness of congruence I had not anticipated.

I was whole.

Yes, I felt the physical pain as well. Emerging from the darkness of anesthesia, I could not but think of the pain of birth, that long journey from egg to life, for I had just been reborn. My birthday was today. It was October 15, 2002, and I was reborn—as a 54-year-old woman.

I turned my head to see Alice in the bed beside me. She was packaged in white just like me, an IV bag hanging over her head. She was asleep. I looked the other way and saw I had the same kind of bag.

Just then the nurse walked into the room carrying a small tray. "Ah, you are awake," she smiled. "How do you feel?"

"I hurt a bit," I croaked.

"Yes, I expect so. But we can take care of that." She walked over to my bedside to check the IV.

"We will give you something for the pain whenever you need it. Just call us. It sometimes makes people nauseous, so we have another injection for that. You understand?"

"Yes, I believe so."

"I have the pain medication for you now, which I will put in your IV line."

She inserted a needle in the line, emptying a large syringe of milky fluid into it. As it proceeded down the line toward my arm, I suddenly felt sick.

"Oh, hell, I think I'm going to throw up!"

"Ah, then you must roll over for me as best you can. . . ."

I struggled to roll onto my right side, offering her my bare left buttock. It hurt to move, especially my chest. She gave me a quick stab, then rolled me back. Almost immediately, it took effect.

"Thank you, that's much better," I said after a moment. "Oh, and the pain medication is starting to work. I feel sleepy."

"Yes, you will rest now for several hours."

"Oh."

I fell instantly asleep.

Alice and I spent two more days in the hospital, then Robert returned with his limo to take us back to the Residence. She and I and two others were sitting around the fireplace when the next round of patients began walking in the door.

Nine days later, I returned to Bellingham. In my purse I carried a signed, stamped, and notarized affidavit from Dr. Brassard's office. One line stood out among all others:

"On October 15, 2002…I successfully completed gender reassignment surgery for Erika J. Shepard and she is now female."

In the days that followed, there developed a feeling of unreality to it, despite the post-operative pain and clear evidence to the contrary. Had it actually happened? After all the years of hiding, of fear, was I finally the woman I so desperately wanted to be?

Yes. And no.

I had started with a dream girl, the perfect girl behind my eyes. She was beautiful and intelligent, able to make her way in the world unfettered, happy and full of joy.

In truth, I was not her. I was not beautiful. My way forward would not be unfettered. It would be strewn with obstacles and fearful resistance from many people as I went, resistance from a culture that did not understand and often did not care to.

But I also was her. I had long accepted the fact that beauty was not within my reach. I did not pass. My voice was too low. I carried masculine traits and mannerisms. But, as I had told Dr. Krympe, I accepted that. Somewhere, walking the long road, I had begun to accept who and what I was. I began to see my way to what I would become. Part man in some ways, part woman in others.

That was okay. That was me. And it was, finally, okay to be me. Nothing special, just another woman crossing the grocery store parking lot, another woman shopping for clothes in the department store.

Simply ordinary, and happy to be alive.

TRANS-FORMATIONS

Forty

Moving On - 2002

"Erika, please eat something," Barb said.

I had returned, rolling off the plane in a wheelchair. She met me at the airport, took me home, and poured me into bed. I had developed an infection that was affecting my whole body with symptoms that were similar to the flu. I was aching and feverish, unable to eat.

"I'll try," I said miserably.

She helped me sit up in bed, adjusted the pillows, then brought a tray of chicken noodle soup with a few crackers. I hadn't been able to keep that much food down in days.

Dr. Brassard's office had been unable to help, and suggested I see my own doctor. I called him, and he prescribed Cipro, an antibiotic. I wasn't too sure which was making me feel worse, infection from surgery or the antibiotic, but I took the dosage as required. For ten days, I lay in bed, curled into a ball, feeling like I might die of complications from a sex change operation. It was almost funny.

On the tenth day, I rose again, unsteady but upright. I had lost ten pounds. After two weeks, I was still weak, but more or less able to function. A few months more, and I was back to normal as Barb and I moved on with our new lives.

"Erika, would you get the mail?"

"Sure, be right back."

Our mailbox was on the road at the end of our driveway, a distance of about 200 feet. Over the years, the old mailbox had leaned back toward the deep ditch behind it as the soil crept downhill. Gotta fix that, I thought for the hundredth time. But not today.

I was wearing my blue dress, the one from the outlet mall, the one acquired in terrified secret so many eons ago.

I walked down the driveway under a crisp spring day, the sun bright in a brilliantly blue sky. I thought about how far I had come—we had come—in the short time since my surgery, and in the long, difficult five years since I handed Barb that letter on a dismal March morning.

And yet, in a way, much had not changed.

We were together. We still loved each other. Barb had asked me to get the mail. I mowed the lawn. Barb did the dishes. We shared the cooking. A thousand little things of no importance to anyone were exactly the same. But they were important. They were the small, insignificant things that formed the brick and mortar of our day-to-day lives.

And we had gained much more than that. We had a new kind of sharing. We shared jewelry. She taught me about makeup. She helped me buy the right clothes. Our new relationship transcended man and wife. Barb had let me into her world, opened her heart, and I was blessed for it.

What would I have done differently, I sometimes wondered? Would I have married Barb?

I had to answer yes.

At the time I thought I was just a pervert. With regular sex, with the love of a good companion, it would go away, right?

Oops.

What the hell did I know, did anyone know, back then? Nothing. I had followed my heart. That's all I could say. I married Barb for love. She married me for love, and she had proven it every day since that horrible day I came out. Yes, there were rough times, angry times. But here we were. Stronger than before.

Was it worth it?

In the worst of times it felt like I was being torn apart, like I was being dismembered from the inside out. I hated myself, I hated what I had done. I wanted to take it all back and start over again. That's all. Can we start again? Please?

But things don't work that way. When I came out, we lost friends. My sisters had ultimately disowned me. They were gone. Perhaps they were never really there in the first place.

I looked up at the sky, puffy white clouds growing and changing even as I watched. It was so clear to me now. I was wearing my favorite blue dress, openly walking down our driveway in the sun to get the mail.

I no longer thought of myself as a pervert.

"Erika, could you help me with something?"

"Of course, what is it?"

"The outside door to Twister's stall is jammed shut, and she's trapped inside. I can't get it open to let her out of the barn. Could you take a look?"

"Sure, no problem." I went to the hallway to get my barn boots, and we headed out the door.

"I'm glad you're feeling better," Barb said as we walked.

"Yes, me too. Thank you for taking such good care of me."

"Oh, that's all right. You know, you seem happier now. I think I always knew you weren't happy, but I thought it was because of me."

I stopped, frozen in a horrible realization—being in the closet inevitably creates pain for everyone, even those you want to protect.

"Oh my god, Barb, I'm so sorry," I said, tears welling up in my eyes. "All those years I was terrified that you would find out, that you would be so disgusted with me that you'd leave. I didn't want that. I've never wanted that. I never meant to hurt you. I'm so sorry."

"Yes, I know that now. I didn't then, and it's only recently that I've begun to understand. But I know it now."

We turned to each other, standing in the driveway in our muddy barn boots and grubby jackets, and hugged. We hugged acknowledging the pain we each had endured, we hugged to say it was okay now, we hugged to promise each other that we would remain together, going forward into whatever life threw at us. Together.

"Okay," I said, voice raspy, "Let's go get Twister."

The exterior doors to the barn stalls were sliding doors on tracks. They hung from an upper wheeled track, while the bottom was in a groove in the cement. The groove often clogged with debris: dirt, horse manure and small rocks. I dug out the groove as best I could, then pulled on the door. It moved a few inches. I pulled again, and managed to get it open about a foot.

I squeezed into the space, placing my back against the door jamb and pushed with both arms. The door moved another foot.

Twister slammed into me like a bulldozer, charging through the narrow opening. She pounded over me, hooves, mud and manure flying. I tumbled under her feet, a rag doll, barely aware of what was happening.

A dazed moment later I found myself lying on my back, not sure if I had been hurt.

I became aware of Barb, screaming as she ran to me, lying in the mud.

"Erika! Erika! Are you all right? Erika!"

I lifted my head, then sat up enough to lean back on my elbows, assessing the damage.

"I'm okay, I'm okay," I said, stunned. "I don't think she broke anything."

"Oh my god, I thought you were hurt, or dead! Are you sure?" She got to me and checked me over, then helped me to my feet.

"Yeah, I think so. I'm gonna be sore and bruised, I think, but I'm okay."

"I don't see anything but a scratch on your head," she said worriedly. "I thought she stomped you as she ran out, maybe killed you."

"I don't know how, but I don't think she stomped me. It was all just a blur."

"You're sure you're okay?"

"Yeah, I think I'm okay. Let's go back to the house. I think I need a long, hot shower and a pain pill."

She had called me Erika, I realized. In a moment of stress, she called me Erika.

Forty-One

Geology Again - 2005

I returned to my job at the call center and continued to send out resumes to mining companies. Wonder of wonders, I found a small company based in a nearby town was advertising for a geologist. It was run by a woman.

I applied, offering my services in any capacity they chose, practically begging for the position. They hired me as an hourly consultant at first, not quite sure if I would work out. Three weeks later I was offered a permanent job with the company, including benefits. The salary, however, was barely two-thirds of what I had earned before transition.

I was getting my first lesson in wage inequality for women.

"So, Erika, we'd like to expand our company, and we think Peru is a place we could do that."

I was meeting with my boss about my role with the company. I had worked for them about six months, including a stint as the temporary chief geologist for their mining operation in Quebec. It was time to branch out.

"We want you to find us a gold property that is for sale or open to a joint venture. Something with potential to expand, but where they just don't have the financial backing they need."

Peru, I thought? I'd better check to see how they treat transgender people down there.

"Okay," I replied, "So what are your parameters? What type of deposit are you looking for? How big, underground or open pit?"

"We're open to about anything that makes economic sense and that we can sell to stockholders as the next big thing for the company," he replied, smiling.

"Ahh, I understand," I said smiling back, ticking off a list on my fingers. "You want excellent tonnage potential, high-grade ore, in a deposit that's easy to mine and has no environmental issues. Oh, and it's just lying around. Got it."

"Ha! Yes, that's exactly what we want!"

"No worries. When do I leave?"

Barb and I had discussed the possibility that I would be travelling again, but we told ourselves we were used to it. We would endure the separation, as before. But we understood the risks were a bit different now, and unpredictable.

Days before I left, I found a disturbing report online. In Lima, a transgender woman had recently been found murdered, her body dumped on the streets of an upscale neighborhood and set on fire.

"She was probably working in the sex trade," I told Barb. "It can't happen to me. I'll be with professionals all the time."

But I was worried. Shit happened to us trannies, I knew. All the time.

❧

Two weeks later, after eighteen exhausting hours of traveling, I arrived at the Lima airport.

The trip had been marred by an attendant on the flight from Atlanta to Lima. For comfort, I wore a dress on the flight, but she repeatedly, and pointedly, referred to me as "sir" every time she handed me peanuts or a drink. Twice I tried to politely correct her, but it was clear she was not going to stop. There was nothing I could do to change her from being a bigot into a decent human being at 35,000 feet.

Arriving in Lima and through customs, I escaped through the exit doors into the terminal. Immediately, I was confronted by a wall of eager taxi drivers, each trying to grab a rich tourist to fleece for the trip into town. I paused to look over the crowd and spotted a professional-looking man standing toward the back holding up a sign that said Shepard.

"I'm Erika Shepard," I said as I approached.

"Ahh, welcome, Erika. I'm Carl. We spoke on the phone?"

"Yes, we did. Pleased to meet you in person," I said as we shook hands.

Carl was an ex-pat Canadian who had lived and worked in Peru for ten years. He was a tall, thin man with a dark tan from many hours in the sun. We had hired him as a consultant, one who was familiar with many of the players in the local mining industry. I would work out of his offices as he contacted companies who had gold properties that might be interested in a deal. He would set up meetings where I would look through their data and discuss, in general terms, what they required. If it looked promising, we'd arrange a visit to the property.

Over the ensuing weeks, various properties were presented to us. Perhaps one in five had the right combination of geology and the potential for a reasonable deal. For those that fit our criteria, we arranged a visit in the field, including properties scattered all over western Peru. Some were in well-known mining districts; a few were in new areas. Two were in the high Andes above 18,000 feet. The trucks we used had bottles of oxygen attached to the back wall of the cab.

As we went about our work, I marveled at how I was being accepted by those we met. I was treated as a professional by the Peruvian engineers and geologists. Clearly, they realized I was transgender the moment I opened my mouth to speak, yet no one made a comment or batted an eye. I enjoyed a higher level of respect in Peru than I encountered in parts of the United States.

There was more. Men held doors for me. I was called Señora Erika, with a deference I had never before experienced. Senior managers of the companies we visited made it point to take me and Carl out for a meal, be it lunch or dinner, and always to nice places. Often they commented on my hair, which had turned blonde over the years.

Sitting in a nice restaurant, the only person in the room with blonde hair and being the center of attention was strange, almost uncomfortable. Yes, they wanted me to buy their property or their company, but it felt like more.

I also noticed that I met no women in positions of management in these companies. I attributed it to the fact that mining and geology careers tend to be populated by men, yet there was a 1950s feel to some of the offices we visited. Women were there as well-dressed assistants and the like, but none received the deference that I received.

Eventually, an exciting property came to us. It was called Minas de Ocoña, located just sixty miles from the coast in southern Peru. It was a gold vein system in granite and had been mined, off and on, since the 1950s. A town of three thousand people huddled around the property. There was no other large employer nearby.

We requested a visit.

The owner was a Peruvian woman named Yolanda. Her husband, a German immigrant after the war, had bought the property and put it into production. They had prospered for many years, but recently he'd passed away. Yolanda struggled to keep it running, but her heart was not in it. She wanted to sell it for six million dollars so she could retire and move to Spain.

"Buenos dias, Señora Yolanda. Me nombre es Erika. ¿Cómo estás?" I said in my bad Spanish.

"Pleased to meet you, Erika," she replied, a big grin on her face as she extended her hand. "I am well, thank you. Welcome to Peru."

"Oh, thank you. I'm glad to be here, and am happy you speak English! My Spanish is poor, as you can see."

"Not a problem, Erika. I am happy to practice my English."

She turned to Carl and shook his hand. A petite lady perhaps in her mid-70s, she was well-dressed and confident. Her ready grin at my Spanish made me like her immediately.

"Our vehicle is outside," she said as the greetings were done. "It is a four-wheel drive. I have asked the former mine manager to join us to do the driving and to answer the technical questions you will have. Will that be all right?"

I looked at Carl, then nodded. "Of course, Yolanda. Thank you for making the arrangements. I think we're ready to go."

"That is good. It is approximately five hours from the airport to the mine site. All is highway except the last 100 kilometers. That part of the road follows the Rio Ocoña and is not paved, but it is well maintained."

On the paved highway, we sped over long stretches of high, dry desert, cut by a few shallow rivers in deep valleys. Only there could agriculture of one type or another flourish. In some places, the farmers grew peppers for paprika, in others, limes. Everywhere else was bone dry. This was the northern reaches of the Atacama Desert, the driest place on Earth.

We eventually stopped in a small coastal town for fuel, then headed inland on a gravel road that ran alongside the Rio Ocoña. Fast, shallow and cold, the river was fed by melting glaciers in the high Andes more than a hundred miles away. The road was cut into the side of the dusty canyon, sometimes wide and easy, sometimes perched and narrow. In most places there was no vegetation to anchor the slopes. The wind would occasionally blow away the sand that held the rocks precariously in place, causing small landslides.

We arrived at the mine site well after the sun had settled behind the ragged, dry hills. Yolanda showed us to rooms in a large dormitory building, saying to me as we parted, "We will tour the mine tomorrow, Erika, if this is okay for you."

"Of course, Yolanda. I will see you at breakfast. Buenas noches."

With that I stepped into my room, pausing for a moment to look around. The bed was a foam pad on a plywood plank.

Just like Alaska, I thought. Just like.

❧

The next morning, we met in the dining hall, where breakfast for senior staff was served to order.

Peru was a class-divided society. The rich, and especially the light-skinned rich, were treated well. The darker skinned workers had to fend for themselves. It was the same everywhere.

What was surprising was the coffee. In a country that exported good coffee in quantity, the only coffee available was freeze-dried instant. Nescafe' was not a brand name here, it was all the coffee there was to be had. Nevertheless, I was grateful to get it.

"I have arranged for the tour of the mine today," Yolanda said, as we lingered over the remains of our breakfast. "The manager will meet us at the mine portal, and we will go inside. There is a rail line that goes under the mountain about half a kilometer, then we will get out and walk. Is that okay for you, Erika?"

"Of course, Yolanda. No problem."

We piled into the truck and headed to the base of the mountain, then up a series of steep switchbacks to the mine portal cut into the hillside a few hundred feet above the valley floor. There, the rail line from the processing facility down below curled up and around the slope, entering the tunnel. Parked at the entrance was an electric mine tug, a "locomotive" used to transport miners and ore back and forth from the depths of the mine. The mine manager, Jorge' was there waiting for us.

"Buenos dias, Jorge'," I said, as we stepped out of the truck.

"Buenos dias, Señora Erika, Señora Yolanda, Señor Carl. ¿Listo para recorrer la mina?"

I stopped for a moment to think through what he had said. Okay, La mina means "the mine," listo means "ready," so he's asking if we are ready to look at the mine.

"Si, Jorge', listo," I replied.

"Muy bien, Señora."

We walked over to a small shack next to the portal. In it were miner's lamps and helmets. Jorge' handed one to me and Carl, then waited to see if we knew what to do with them.

I strapped the heavy battery and belt around my waist, cinching it tightly and shifting the battery to ride over my tailbone. Adjusting it for size, I donned the miner's helmet. I then draped the cord and light over my shoulder, checking the light to be sure it was in proper working order.

"Listo, amigo," I said, looking back at him. He smiled, realizing I had done this before. Carl and Yolanda did the same.

He herded us to the locomotive where we boarded, sitting in benches in front of the driver's station, which was located at the back where Jorge' stood at the controls of the locomotive.

"There are some low spots in the tunnel," Yolanda said as we started to roll. "Watch for your head."

"Gracias, will do," I replied.

We entered the tunnel. The daylight dwindled behind us as we moved into the darkness, trundling along in the cool, damp air, lit only by the headlight of the locomotive and our helmet lamps.

A half-mile or so into the mountain we entered a wide area, well lit by neon fixtures hanging from the rock ceiling. It was the loading area where the ore was collected from other parts of the mine and shipped outside.

"It is here we get off," Yolanda said as we slowed down, "and go to see the veins."

We followed Yolanda and Jorge' as they moved away from the light, our miner's lamps casting pale yellow beams into the darkness as we walked. There's nothing like the dark of a mine or a cave, I thought. It is thick, absolutely black—it almost has a texture.

We continued through the tunnels in the darkness for perhaps ten minutes, moving through occasional shallow puddles of dark silty water on the tunnel floors. Then Yolanda and Jorge' stopped at a side passage that intersected the tunnel.

"Erika, this is the place where the vein is widest," she said.

I walked into the passage and looked up. The vein was clear to see, reflecting the light of our lamps. Nearly five feet wide, the white milky quartz was streaked with fragments of the granitic wall rock and traces of reddish-yellow iron oxide. It extended the width of the passage, disappearing into the darkness ahead of us. I moved to the tunnel wall to examine the edge of the vein.

"Is there any ore-grade material in the vein walls?" I asked. Yolanda turned to Jorge' and asked him in Spanish.

"No, señora," He replied. " No oro en la pared."

"And the vein width? What is the average vein width, and the narrowest vein you've encountered?"

Yolanda again translated.

"The average vein is approximately two feet wide, but they can be as narrow as a few inches."

"And the grade of the ore? Is it consistent?"

"Yes, it is consistent at fifteen grams per ton, no matter how wide the vein is."

Fifteen grams per ton equaled nearly half an ounce per ton. That's good, I thought, if that's true, and the assays are reliable.

"Okay. Señora, y señor, with your permission I would like to collect some samples here and in other parts of the vein. Specifically, I would like to get some representative samples of wall rock, and channel samples across narrow veins and wide ones to confirm they are consistent. I'd also like to submit some test samples to your lab for analysis. Would that be all right?"

"Of course, Erika. If you wish, we will have someone come to the mine to take the samples for you, under your supervision, of course."

"Muchas gracias, Señora. That is kind of you."

I was excited about what we saw. If the samples were good, if the conditions were as described by Yolanda and Jorge', if the veins could be mapped on the surface, then there was potential. The only way to tell would be to drill. It was narrow-vein mining, which was always a risky venture, but the company had experience in that, and the Peruvian miners were known for their skill in working in such environments.

Okay, I decided. This was it. This one has a chance of being the right property for the company, one we can sell to investors and perhaps even produce some gold.

Two months later, I was back at Minas de Ocoña. The company had bought the property. I returned to plan the exploration drilling program needed to test the veins for ore reserve estimates.

"They want me?" I said, looking up from the maps at my desk. "Are you sure?"

"Si, Señora Erika," Miguel, our interpreter and new office manager replied. "The mayor and council would like you to honor us by raising the Peru flag at our Independence Day celebration today. I come for you at one o'clock, if that would be okay."

"But why me, Miguel?"

"Señora, you have brought your company to Ocoña to re-open our gold mine. That makes jobs for many people in our town, and we want to show appreciation. Please say you will come, Señora."

"I was just doing my job, Miguel."

"Yes, that may be so, but please come."

"Okay, amigo, I certainly can't refuse. I'll come."

Miguel left to inform the mayor. I stared at the door for a long moment after he was gone, then got up and went outside.

It was a wonder to me. They wanted to honor me. Me, a gringa geologist. More, a transgender gringa geologist.

In the shade of the concrete office building was a bench. An old, wooden bench that had seen many occupants, many sittings such that the dark wood was polished with use. I sat and looked out over the valley.

It was all dry dust and rock, baked yellow-hard in the perpetual sun by day and freeze-dried by night under unlimited stars. Steep, ragged slopes dominated the landscape, slopes that would take half a day and a gallon of water to climb. It was special, unique in its risks and its rewards, as had been all of the places I had worked, all the roads I had traveled.

I also pondered how very lucky I had been. There were so many others—straight or gay, transgender or not—who never had the opportunities, who never received the support that I enjoyed.

Yet we all struggle to become our true selves at some point in our lives. But we cannot do it alone.

When Miguel returned to the office, I went back inside. It was time to raise the flag—for all of us.

Forty-Two

Crystallization - 2011

"Thank you for your attention, and I'll be glad to take any questions you might have."

I was speaking to a Sex and Gender class of about fifty students in a lecture hall at Western Washington University. I had given many such talks by this time, to college classes large and small. I received a polite round of applause, then a few hands went up.

"Umm, like, you know, if it's not too personal, how does the surgery work?"

"No, that's not too personal at all. It's called Penile Inversion. It's like this."

I raised my left hand, making a fist with my index finger extended. I explained that the surgeon enters from behind the scrotum and removes the testes and continues up into the penis, removing most of the spongiosum—the tissue in the penis that engorges with blood during an erection. They then turn around and create an opening in the perineum. Finally, the surgeon inverts the remaining penile and scrotal tissue and anchors it inside the body through that opening, creating a neo-vagina and clitoral area. The urethra is also re-routed so that we can pee. The surgery is designed to maintain a good blood supply to the tissue so it can heal and remain healthy, and the nerve endings of the penis remain intact.

"That means, yes, we can orgasm," I said.

A nervous titter of laughter went through the class.

"Hey, it's important," I quipped, smiling. More laughter would release some of the tension at asking such questions, I knew.

"How do you like being a woman?"

"You know, I am happy with where I am now. I don't actually consider myself to be completely a woman, though. I'll never menstruate, never have children, I've missed out on a lifetime of girlfriends and sleepovers and all the things that girls experience growing up. I was never fully a man, either. I played the part, but it was an act. I'm somewhere in between. I don't pass as a woman; I have a man's build, a low voice. But that's okay. The process has allowed me to come to terms with who and what I am. I'm okay with that."

Another hand went up.

"What are you and your wife doing now?" a young lady asked.

I paused for a moment before answering, then spoke. "Ah, yes. What now. Sadly, my Barb passed away last year from lung cancer."

The room was silent.

I looked directly at the student who had asked the question.

"Thank you for asking that question. Really.

"It leads me to the last point I want to make today. I'd like to close with something Barb said to me. It was after she had asked me to move back into the house. Remember, it was Erika moving in, not Rich, so in a way we had to get to know each other all over again.

"One day she turned to me and said, 'I think I always knew you were unhappy, but I thought it was because of me.'"

I stopped, letting the words sink in, then went on.

"Those words struck me in the gut, and I've thought about them ever since. I've come to realize that when we hide in the closet we think we are protecting ourselves and, we believe, protecting our friends and families from the shame or trauma of finding out about us. No one will know, we desperately hope. No one will ever suspect.

"Barb's words made it clear to me. They will know. Our family will sense when we are in pain, our friends will wonder if, at some unspoken level, we are not quite truthful with them. The people in our lives that know us, that care about us? At some intuitive level they will feel it. And they will likely think it's their fault.

"After Barb and I got back together, our relationship had changed. Sex was no longer part of the equation, but we had found something else, something much more solid and enduring. We found love, a love based in truth.

"No hiding, no secrets, just the truth. I could finally be myself without risk. She could do the same. We knew without doubt that even if we disagreed, we would still be together the next morning. That no matter what happened, we would be there for each other. After all, we had just been through hell and survived, hadn't we? So, after all we had gone through, her death felt so unfair, so wrong.

"So here is what I have learned: accept yourself, and you will be accepted. Have respect, and you will be respected. Gay or straight, trans or not, we all need to be loved and to love ourselves.

"It is the same for everyone, this fear. To one degree or another, we all must face the prospect of coming out, of letting ourselves be true to who we are. We cannot spend our entire lives living up to other people's expectations. We must, somehow, find a way to live up to our own.

"Ultimately, when you face this challenge and succeed, you will gain something profound. That thing is unconditional love—love of the important people around you. Love of yourself.

"And believe me, you never know how much time you have left to find it."

ACKNOWLEDGMENTS

"It's all about me!" my friends and I joke to each other as we sip a glass of wine, sharing our day-to-day challenges and triumphs. Yes, perhaps writing a memoir about yourself is, as they say, a supreme act of ego. The whole darn book is all about me, right?

Not really.

It's about my mother, Margaret, doing her level best to give her young son the earth and the sky—and succeeding. It's about my wife, Barbara, who showed her tortured husband the true meaning of unconditional love.

It's about the friendships that sustain us. There's my friend, Barbara Gobus, who in her quiet way revealed herself to be a secret saint and speaker of Proper English, thank you very much. Tea anyone? And her husband Spence Gobus, the honest man who cooks for fun and says what he thinks. There's my dear friend Liz Weber, she of the razor-sharp mind, gentle editing, and frequent loving praise. These are the kind of friends that make life worth living.

I also owe a debt of gratitude to Redd Becker and Beth Stickley, my writing group comrades-in-arms. They, too, poked and prodded this amateur, offering a different perspective, a better turn of phrase, or a useful thought hidden from my narrow view. It helped immensely, my friends.

Meet Jill McCabe Johnson from *The Artful Editor*, a wonderful young woman of letters who lives and breathes the written word. She offered insights into the craft of writing. I took what I could, but did not follow all of her advice. If I had, it might have been better, but it would not have become the book I needed to write. She understood, and made that okay.

Finally, I must thank Joann Eisenbrandt, who with dogged determination and attention to detail hammered out the book you hold in your hands.

So, it's all about me, isn't it?

Not really. Underneath the geology adventures and self-absorption, this is a book about connection, about the people in our lives that help make us who we are. We can't do it alone, this coming to terms with ourselves. We need each other, no matter what our path might be.